Sinclare Kelburn

The Divinity of Our Lord Jesus Christ Asserted and Proved

And the connexion of this doctrine with practical religion, pointed out, in

five sermons

Sinclare Kelburn

The Divinity of Our Lord Jesus Christ Asserted and Proved
And the connexion of this doctrine with practical religion, pointed out, in five sermons

ISBN/EAN: 9783337114121

Printed in Europe, USA, Canada, Australia, Japan

Cover: Foto ©Lupo / pixelio.de

More available books at **www.hansebooks.com**

THE DIVINITY

OF OUR

Lord Jesus Christ

ASSERTED AND PROVED,

AND THE

CONNEXION OF THIS DOCTRINE

WITH

PRACTICAL RELIGION,

POINTED OUT,

IN FIVE SERMONS.

By SINCLARE KELBURN, A.B.
Of Belfast, Ireland.

In the beginning was the WORD, *and the* WORD *was with* GOD *and the* WORD *was* GOD. *The* SAME *was in the beginning with* GOD. *All things were made by* HIM, *and without* HIM *was not any thing made, that was made.* JOHN 1st. CHAP.

And without Controversy, great is the mystery of Godliness; GOD WAS MANIFEST IN THE FLESH. Tim. iii. 16.

PHILADELPHIA:
Printed by and for W. W. WOODWARD, No. 36, Chesnut-street, south side, green sign Franklin's Head.

1795.

Philadelphia, April 28, 1795.

THE discourses of the Rev. Mr. SINCLAIR KELBURN, upon the *Divinity of our Lord and Saviour Jesus Christ*, contain a clear statement and judicious defence of that essential doctrine of Christianity. They are written in a very good style and engaging manner, and they are contained within so small a compass as to be attainable by the poor. It is with pleasure therefore, that I take this opportunity to recommend them to the attention and perusal of all my fellow Christians; they may serve as an useful remedy against the poison of corrupt principles contained in some pamphlets lately published in this city, which though extremely superficial, are, however, dangerous to those who have not read much upon the subject. Persons who have not leisure to read, or ability to purchase Mr. Gowan's masterly, witty, and victorious refutation of Dr. Priestley; or Fuller's fifteen letters, filled with unanswerable arguments against the Socinian heresy, may find in these discourses what will be sufficient to satisfy every candid and enquiring mind, that JESUS CHRIST is the eternal SON of GOD; from whence we justly infer, that his atonement is an infinite satisfaction to divine justice in the forgiveness of sin, and that moral evil therefore, is infinite in its malignity and demerit.

JOHN B. SMITH, A. M.
Minister of the 3d Presbyterian Church,
PHILADELPHIA.

N. B. It is hoped that the opposers of the DIVINITY of our SAVIOUR will be candid enough to regard the arguments contained in the books above mentioned, as those on which judicious Christians rely for a defence of their principles, rather than on the weak and obscure, though well-intended answer to Dr. Priestley's appeal, which has been lately published here. J. B. S.

SERMON FIRST.

John, 20th Chap. 28th Verse.

And Thomas answered and said unto him, my Lord and my God.

THE incredulity of this Disciple respecting the Resurrection of the Lord Jesus, may justly be considered as a circumstance which tends to corroborate the evidence in favor of that most important and glorious event. The Apostle's incredulity was overcome by the most incontestible evidence, for he was made an eye witness, and more than an eye witness, that the Lord was risen indeed; and having all his doubts removed, he acknowledged his risen Saviour, and made a confession of his faith in him as his Lord, and his God.

My design in the following discourses, is to assert and vindicate the important doctrine of Christ's divinity;

nity; and this I will endeavour to do in a plain and familiar manner, and it is my prayer to the God of truth, that his holy fpirit would guide and lead us into all truth, and that the eyes of our underftandings being opened, our prejudices removed, and our wills renewed, we may be enabled to perceive the glory of Jefus Chrift, and chearfully to embrace the truth as it is in him.

It will be eafily perceived, that as the doctrine above mentioned is entirely a doctrine of revelation, a doctrine not to be difcovered by the light of Nature, fo all the arguments in its favour are to be Scriptural, and derived from that revelation in which this doctrine is fuppofed to be afferted; in fhort, the grand queftion is this, is the doctrine of Chrift's divinity revealed in the word of God; is it a Scripture doctrine? And therefore it muft be obvious, that the following difcourfes are addreffed to thofe only who believe or profefs to believe the holy Scriptures.

We fuppofe it will be granted that all the attributes of God are, in the fenfe they are afcribed to him, incommunicable; that they are effential to the Divine nature, infeparable from it, and can neither belong or be afcribed to any other nature; and therefore it would be blafphemy to afcribe the Divine attributes and perfections to a finite being, to one who is not really and truly God. If then it can be demonftrated that the divine, infinite, and adorable perfections are in Scripture afcribed to the fon of Chrift Jefus,

Jesus, this conclusion must necessarily follow, that if the Scriptures are the word of that God who cannot lie, Jesus Christ the son of God, is our Lord and our God, really and truly God.

It is proposed in the first place, to shew that the Divine attributes are in Scripture ascribed to the son Christ Jesus.

Secondly, we shall shew that the glorious and incommunicable name of God, JEHOVAH, is ascribed to the same person, and that he is called by this name.

Thirdly, we will quote and illustrate some passages of Scripture in which Jesus Christ is expressly called God.

In the fourth place it will be proved, that Jesus Christ is the object of adoration and religious worship.

Lastly, we will give a general answer to objectors, and point out the practical use of the doctrine.

First then, let us shew that the Divine perfections, the essential attributes of God, and all his attributes are essential, are ascribed to Jesus Christ the son of God. And to begin with the attribute, Eternal, we find it ascribed unto the son of God, not merely because he shall exist for ever, but because he really did exist from all eternity. The Prophet asserts the eternity of the Son, when he says, *his goings forth have been from of old, from everlasting* *,
for

---

* Micah v. 2.

for he that acts from everlasting, that is from all eternity, exists from all eternity, because action supposes existence. But do these words of the Prophet relate to the Son of God? The evangelist Matthew will answer the question, and shew us that the words of the Prophet relate to Christ.

When Jesus was born in Bethlehem of Judea, in the days of Herod the king, there came wise men from the East to Jerusalem saying, where is he that is born king of the Jews? For we have seen his star in the East, and are come to worship him. Herod made the same inquiry but not with the same view; he demanded of the chief priests and elders where Christ should be born, *and they said unto him, in Bethlehem of Judea, for thus it is written by the Prophet, and thou Bethlehem in the land of Juda, art not the least among the princes of Juda, for out of thee shall come a Governor that shall rule my people Israel**. It is evident that the Prophet and the Evangelist speak of one and the same person who should be ruler in Israel, even the great Messiah, whose goings forth, says Micah, have been from everlasting; therefore he that came out of Bethlehem Ephratah, that is, Christ, was from everlasting.

This same attribute is ascribed to the Son, by the evangelist John, and he wrote his gospel at a period

---

* Matth. ii. 1. 6.

riod when the myftery of iniquity had begun to work; for the divinity and the incarnation of the fon of God was denied by fome even in the days of the Apoftles. We confider it as a wife and well ordered difpenfation of Providence, that many truths of the everlafting gofpel were controverted, at a time when the enemies of the truth could be contradicted, and refuted by fome of the Apoftles in perfon, by which means we have an apoftolical decifion in favour of thefe doctrines, which is as valid this day as ever it was. St. John fets his face againft the errors of the times, and refutes them in his epiftles and in his gofpel, which he begins with an exprefs declaration of Chrift's eternity; *in the beginning was the Word, and the Word was with God, and the word was God, the fame was in the beginning with God, all things were made by him, and without him was not any thing made that was made**. Let us exercife our reafon impartially upon thefe words of the Evangelift. If by the beginning, we fhould underftand the commencement of time, then it is plain that the Logos, or Word, did not begin to exift when time began or commenced; he exifted before time, before creation, before any thing was created, and enjoyed glory with God before the world was. As the Evangelift afferts that the Logos made all things, fo of neceffity he muft have had an exiftence prior to the things that were by him created and made; he muft have exifted before the creation of all things, and of courfe he is not a created

---

* John, i. Chap. 1, 2. Ver.

created being; the Creator of all things is uncreated and eternal. We shall have occasion hereafter to speak of the Son as Creator of all things visible and invisible, and of his *eternal power and god-head*, demonstrated by the works of creation, and therefore I shall at present only insist upon a few passages of Scripture which are sufficient to prove the eternity of the Son of God, I think there can be no doubt but the eternity of God is clearly asserted in these words of the Prophet, *thus saith the Lord the King of Israel, and his Redeemer the Lord of Hosts, I am the first and I am the last, and besides me there is no God**. It is of no moment, as to the present question, whether these words are spoken by the Father or by the Son; it is sufficient if these words, the first and the last, are expressive of the attribute, Eternal, and that they are so need not be proved. Now the same words are used by the inspired writers, when they speak of the Son of God; Jesus is *Alpha and Omega, the beginning and the end*†, Jesus is *the first and the last*‡, and therefore the attribute of eternity belongs to him; he claims it as his undoubted right.

Jesus asserted his eternity in a conversation with the Jews, who were offended at him, because he said that Abraham saw his day and rejoiced; Jesus said unto them, *verily, verily, I say unto you, before Abraham was, I am*§: he does not say before Abraham was I was, but, I am, and thus he claims the attribute of eternity, and asserts his eternity, in assuming

---

* Isaiah, xliv 6. † Rev. ii 6--i. 8. ‡ Rev. i. 18. § John viii. 58.

suming the name of the eternal God, the great I AM. This is the name of God, I AM THAT I AM. *Thus shalt thou say unto the children of Israel, I AM hath sent me unto you.**

As God is eternal, so also is he unchangeable; he that exists from all eternity, must exist forever unchangeably the same; wherefore the Psalmist singing the praises of the true God, the eternal and unchangeable God, addresses him in the following sublime and beautiful language, *Of old hast thou laid the foundations of the Earth, and the Heavens are the works of thy hands. They shall perish, but thou shalt endure; yea all of them shall wax old like a garment; as a vesture shalt thou change them and they shall be changed. But thou art the same, and thy years shall have no end* †. The Apostle in his epistle to the Hebrews, shews us that these words of the Psalmist, relate to the son of God, and though in the mouth of the Prophet, they may be considered as praise addressed to the son of God, yet the Apostle shews us that they are the words of the Father addressed to the Son, as a full declaration of his Godhead. The Psalmist, in spirit, repeats the words of the Father to the Son, and in these words sings the praises of the eternal and unchangeable Creator, who is *the same yesterday, and to day, and forever* ‡. If Jesus is the same yesterday and to day and forever, he is the unchangeable

* Exod. 3. 14. † 102 Psalm. ‡ Heb. xiii. 8.

able God; and that he is the same yesterday, and to-day, and for ever, is asserted by the Apostle.

The next attribute of the Divine nature to be considered, is that of Omniprefence, and it belongs to the true God and to him alone. *Am I a God at hand, faith the Lord, and not a God afar off? Can any hide himself in secret places that I shall not see him, faith the Lord? Do not I fill Heaven and Earth, faith the Lord?* Now Christ asserts his Omniprefence in his discourse with Nicodemus, *No man, faith Jesus, hath ascended up to Heaven but he that came down from Heaven, even the Son of Man which is in Heaven.* The body of Jesus could not be in Heaven and on Earth at one and the same time, and therefore we must understand these words *(which is in heaven)* as relating to that Nature which fills Heaven and Earth, and is every where present, and we conclude that Jesus is possessed of this nature, and that he is really and truly Omnipresent. The glorified body of Jesus, is in Heaven, his body is not Omnipresent, yet Jesus is present with his church on Earth, and with his church in Heaven; the whole church is the mystical body of Christ, *The fulness of him that filleth all in all** : Here the Apostle says that Christ, filleth all in all, compare this expression with what God says of himself, by the mouth of the Prophet, *Do not I fill Heaven and Earth, faith the Lord?*
It

---

* Eph. i. 23.

It was the promise of God to Israel, that he would be present with his people; *In all places where I record my name, will I come unto thee and bless thee.* And if this be a good proof of God's Omnipresence, as it certainly is, then the promise of the son of God to the church, when he says, *Where two or three are met together in my name, there am I in the midst of them**, must be as good a proof of his Omnipresence. But these words of our Lord will be taken by some in a figurative sense; as if Christ meant no more by his promise, than that he would countenance and bless his assembled people, or that he is present with them by his authority. Even in this sense of the words we find an argument to prove his Omniscience; and we grant that Christ is present with his people in this figurative sense; but we contend, that he is actually present with his people every where, and that he is in the midst of them. He does not say, when two or three are met together in my name, then I am with them; but he says, *where* and *there*, and *in the midst:* which words relate to place, not time. But it may be asked, if Christ is thus in the midst of his people by virtue of his Omnipresence, is he not therefore necessarily present? And then how can his words be considered as a promise, or his presence a privilege to his people? I answer that the same objection, if it has any weight, lies against the promise of God to his people; under

* Matth. xviii. 20.

the Old Testament dispensation; yet there can be no doubt but that promise was considered as a very precious one, and that privilege as a very exalted one.

But the above figurative interpretation involves those that deny the Ubiquity of Christ, in difficulties insurmountable. For to be in the midst of the people, has some meaning, and if it means no more than the authority and blessings of Christ's kingdom, if it only signifies his favour and good-will, then Christ's authority over his church must be granted; it must be granted that his people are in the way of their duty when they assemble in his name; that they receive some peculiar advantage by doing so: and that Christ, some way or other, is employed in obtaining for them a favourable answer to their prayers: their requests shall be granted, because Christ is in the midst of them. Why so? Suppose we should answer, because Christ is their advocate and intercessor, and because he offers up and presents the prayers of the saints with incense; this though it is not all that our Saviour's words mean, yet it is part of the truth, and sufficient to prove that Jesus is entitled to the attribute of Omniscience. For if Jesus is concerned in obtaining for his people a favourable answer to their prayers, then he must know when they pray, and what their prayers are; he must know that his people are met in his name; and

and whatever good he may be supposed to do for his people, whatever he means, by being in the midst of them, he must at least know who are his people, and who are not; the Lord knoweth them that are his, which is an argument that he is Omniscient. There is nothing gained therefore by evading the proof of Christ's Omnipresence, contained in the above-mentioned passages of Scripture; for if his Omniscience be either granted or proved, as shall be done in what follows, it is of no advantage to the cause, to deny his Omnipresence.

That the attribute, Omniscient, belongs to Jesus Christ, is clearly asserted by the Apostle Peter, when addressing himself to Jesus, he uses these remarkable words: *Lord thou knowest all things, thou knowest that I love thee.* Was this a flattering compliment, or the real truth? Who will venture to assert the former? If then the words of the Apostle are true, and that they are true we have this evidence, namely, that Jesus did not reprove Peter, but on the contrary approved of his declaration, by immediately giving him charge to feed his sheep; I say if the words of Peter are true, as they certainly are, then they contain this true proposition, that Christ knoweth all things. Again, it is said of Christ, that *he needed not that any should testify of man; for he knew what was in man**. It is expressly said that *he knew*

---

* John ii. 24, 25.

knew all men; he knew their hearts, and he was acquainted with their secret thoughts, reasonings, surmises, and murmurings; *Jesus knew from the beginning who they were that believed not, and who should betray him* *.

If any should make light of these testimonies, there is a declaration of the Lord Jesus, which is not only perfectly decisive, but of a most awful and alarming nature. *All the Churches shall know, that I am he which searcheth the reins and hearts; and I will give unto every one of you according to his works* †. Compare these words with what God says by the mouth of the Prophet, *I the Lord search the heart, I try the reins, even to give unto every man according to his ways* ‡. It is most evident that the person who speaks thus, by the Prophet, is the all-wise God; it is his prerogative to search the hearts, and try the reins of the children of men: as Solomon declares at the dedication of the Temple: *Hear thou in Heaven thy dwelling place, and forgive and do, and give to every man according to his ways; whose heart thou knowest, for thou, even thou only, knowest the hearts of all the children of men.* §

As the Lord Jesus is the person who shall judge the world in righteousness; he must therefore be possessed

* John vi. 64. † Rev. ii. 23. ‡ Jer. xvii. 10.
§ Kings viii. 39.

fessed of infinite knowledge: for how can he judge righteously if he does not know the hearts of all the children of men? If he will render unto every one according to the deeds done in the body; if he will give unto every one according to his ways; he must know every individual that shall stand before his tribunal: he must know their works and their ways, their actions, their words and their thoughts; nothing must be hid from him; he must be the searcher of hearts indeed: and that he is so, is asserted by himself, and by his Apostle under the influence of his holy spirit. *The Word of God is quick and powerful, and sharper than any two edged sword, piercing, even to the dividing asunder of soul and spirit, and of the joints and marrow, and is a discerner of the thoughts and intents of the heart; neither is there any creature that is not manifest in his sight; but all things are naked and opened unto the eyes of him with whom we have to do**. Another attribute of the Divine nature is Omnipotence, or Almighty power; he that is Omnipotent is God; our God is the mighty God of Jacob, the most mighty, the Almighty. Now if this attribute is ascribed to Jesus the Son of God, it must follow as a just conclusion, that he is possessed of that nature to which this attribute is essential; and that it is ascribed to the Son of God we have abundant evidence. Thus saith the evangelical prophet: *Unto us a child is born, unto us a son is given, and the government shall be upon his shoulder; and his name*

---

* Heb. iv. 12. 13.

name shall be called Wonderful, Councellor, the mighty God, the everlasting Father, the Prince of Peace* and the Psalmist thus addresses the Son of God, *gird thy sword upon thy thigh, O most Mighty, with thy glory and thy majesty; and in thy majesty ride prosperously, because of truth and meekness, and righteousness; and thy right hand shall teach thee terrible things.*† When the Apostle says, that Christ *is able even to subdue all things to himself*,‡ he ascribes unto him almighty power, for that alone is able to subdue all things; and we may safely conclude that the Son of God is Almighty, *for by him were all things created that are in Heaven and that are in Earth, visible and invisible, whether they be thrones, or dominions, or principalities, or powers, all things were created by him and for him, and he is before all things, and by him all things consist.*§ In these words we have a full proof of Christ's omnipotence, for creation is the work of almighty power. The Apostle says, that the invisible things of God, *from the creation of the world are clearly seen, being understood by the things that are made, even his eternal power and godhead.*‖ The things that are made demonstrate the being and existence of the invisible God; they are a bright and glorious demonstration of his eternal power and godhead. God is invisible,

---

* Isaiah, ix. 6. † Psalm, 45. ‡ Philippians, iii. 21.
§ Coloss. i. 16. ‖ Rom. i. 20.

and his power is invisible in itself, it can only be seen in its effects, the mighty works it has done. The things that are made, are the mirrors in which we behold the rays of divine and infinite power, they prove that there is a God, because they prove that there is an eternal, creating power; and shall they prove the eternal power of God, and leave it doubtful whether this power is infinite, or almighty? No, there can be no doubt in this case, the power that is eternal is infinite, almighty; there can be no such thing as an eternal imperfection, whoever is eternal is all perfect. Thus the light of nature renders the conduct of the Heathens inexcusable, when professing themselves to be wise, they became fools; and changed the glory of the incorruptible God, into an image made like to corruptible man. How inexcusable then are they that refuse to glorify the Son of God, who is the Creator of all things visible and invisible! They rob him of the glory of his works, and refuse to give him that praise which is due to the Great Creator, even the God who made them. But is there less power required to uphold all things than to create all things? Surely not; now Christ is said to uphold all things by the word of his power; he is not only before all things, but by him all things consist, which is as much as to say, that *in him we live, and move, and have our being.* It cannot be denied that the Son of God created all things; but some will endeavour to evade the force

of

of this argument, by saying that the Son created all things, only as an instrument and by communicated power. We answer, that the visible creation, the things that are made, are a clear demonstration of eternal power and godhead: and can Eternal and Almighty power, can infinity, be communicated to a finite being*? Can an instrument exercise Almighty power? But farther, if the Son is an instrumental creator, is this instrument eternal or not? If he is eternal, I must ascribe unto him absolute perfection, and then he is possessed of infinite power: If he is not eternal, then he is a created being; and yet the Creator of all things visible and invisible, an instrumental self-creating Creator and creature; but this is a most palpable absurdity. Is it not more rational, seeing we must acknowledge that Christ is the Creator of all things visible and invisible, and that he upholds all things by the word of his power, and that all things were made by him and for him; I say, is it not more rational to confess that he is possessed of Eternal and Almighty power, and that this power was exercised by him in the work of creation, than to have recourse to such a lame hypothesis? But that Christ is possessed of Almighty power we cannot deny, unless we are disposed to contradict the Apostle when he asserts, that in Jesus *dwelleth all the fullness of the Godhead bodily* †.

* Note, Christ is a Creature if he is not God Almighty.
† Colossians, ii. 9.

There are indeed, two texts of Scripture, which are confidered by fome, as an argument in favour of the above-mentioned hypothefis of inftrumental creation; the firft, is the ninth verfe of the third chapter of the epiftle to the Ephefians, viz. *And to make all men fee what is the fellowſhip of the myſtery, which from the beginning of the world hath been hid in God who created all things by Jeſus Chriſt.* The fecond paffage is in the epiftle to the Hebrews, firft chapter and fecond verfe, viz. *by whom alſo he made the Worlds.* The firft of thefe texts relates, we prefume, to the new birth, the new creation, the renovation of the hearts of men; in this fenfe the word create, is ufed in other places of this Epiftle, as is fufficiently obvious; and the word created, may be taken in this fenfe, in the Text above quoted. In the divine economy of falvation, the Father is faid to do feveral things by his Son, acting in the mediatorial capacity; but this is no proof that the Son is inferior to the Father; nay, what the Son does in this capacity is a proof of his almighty power. As to the other text, *by whom alſo he made the worlds,* fome have endeavoured to explain it in the fame way; but I have no objection to confider it as relating to the work of creation in a natural fenfe, though I do not pretend to fay that it is neceffary fo to do; but admitting that both thefe paffages relate to the work of creation in a natural fenfe,

D what

what do they prove? They do not prove that the Son is a creature; do they prove that the power by him exercised in creating all things, creating the worlds, is not Almighty? Do they prove that it is not eternal, and that the things that are made, are not a demonstration of his eternal power and Godhead? It is sufficient to prove the Almighty power of Jesus Christ, that all things were created by him: if he exercises almighty power, then he is almighty.

Though we may not be able to asertain the precise meaning of the Apostle in the above two texts, yet we can plainly see that they do not support an absurd hypothesis, and that they do not contradict, because they were not intended to contradict those declarations of scripture, in which the Son is directly addressed, and spoken of, as the creator of all things.

Can we think that the Apostle meant to deny the omnipotence of him that laid the foundations of the earth? Can we think that the Psalmist did not praise the Almighty Creator, when he says, *of old hast thou laid the foundations of the Earth, and the Heavens are the work of thy hands?* Which words are applied to Christ by the Apostle in the Epistle to the Hebrews; yea, they are to be considered as addressed to the Son by the Father, saying, *Thou Lord in the beginning hast laid the foundation of the Earth, and the Heavens are the work of thine hands.*

Farther,

Farther, he that made all things, made them for himself. Creation gives him a complete property in the creatures, they are his because he made them; *the Heavens are thine, the earth also is thine; as for the world and the fulness thereof thou hast founded them:* Now all things were made by the Son, *and for him, and by him all things consist. All things were made by him, and without him was not any thing made that was made.*

The Resurrection of the Dead, at the coming, and by the power of Christ, will be a glorious demonstration of his almighty power; and as the scripture assures us that the dead shall be raised, and that Christ is the person who will raise the dead, change our vile bodies, and fashion them like unto his glorious body, *according to the working whereby he is able even to subdue all things to himself**; So we have here full evidence of his almighty power.

Moses, in his account of the creation, says, that the ELOHIM created the heaven and the earth; this word ELOHIM is in the plural number, and construed with a verb in the singular number; and this is no obscure intimation that the work of creation was performed by more persons than one; and that these are one God. The ELOHIM said, let us make man in our Image. There is only one God,
but

* Philip. iii. 21.

but in the Godhead there are three distinct persons; these persons are called the Father, the Son, and the Holy Ghost. These three are one God. *For there are three that bear record in Heaven, the Father, the Word, and the Holy Ghost, and these three are one.* Though the authenticity of this text has been controverted, yet it has not been proved that it is spurious; on the contrary, there are many evidences of its authenticity; but without it, there is Scripture enough to prove the doctrine of the ever-blessed Trinity. The Father is called Jehovah, the Son is called Jehovah, and the Spirit is called Jehovah, yet Jehovah the living and true God, is one God. That the Father is Creator, none will deny; that the Son is Creator, and that the Spirit is Creator, is not to be denied without contradicting the holy Scriptures; and though we do not pretend to know the system of order, observed by the Divine persons in the Godhead, in the work of creation, for the ways and works of God are unsearchable, yet we know that creation is the work of the Father, Son and Holy Ghost; that the things that are made, are a demonstration of eternal power, almighty power and Godhead, and that, therefore, the power of the Son, which we here particularly intend to prove, is eternal and almighty.

If what has been said concerning the power of Christ, as evidenced in the works of creation and providence, if his having created all things, and his present upholding all things by the word of his power, and his being able even to subdue all things to himself, should seem precarious, and insufficient to prove that he is intitled to the attribute Almighty; there are many texts of Scripture in which this attribute is directly ascribed to the Son of God.

In the first chapter of the Revelation of John, we find these remarkable words: *I am Alpha and Omega, the beginning and the ending faith the Lord, which is and which was, and which is to come, the Almighty.* In these words are contained the divine attributes of eternity and omnipotence; of this there can be no doubt; the only question is, who is the person, whose words John repeats? They are the words of Jesus. *Who is the faithful witness, the first begotten of the dead, and the prince of the kings of the earth:* they are the words of that Saviour, whom John worshipped, saying, *unto him that loved us, and washed us from our sins in his own blood, and hath made us kings and priests unto God and his Father; to him be glory and dominion for ever and ever, amen.* The coming of this glorious person is proclaimed, and his dignity is asserted in the words which here follow; I am Alpha and Omega, the beginning and the ending, faith the Lord, which is, and which was, and which is to come, the Almighty. The Apostle tells us the place and time, where, and when, he saw his vision, it was in the

Isle

Isle of Patmos, and on the Lord's day. *I was in the spirit on the Lord's day, and heard behind me a great voice, as of a trumpet, saying, 1 am Alpha and Omega, the first and the last. And I turned to see the voice that spake with me,* (that is, I turned to see the person who uttered the voice) *and being turned, I saw seven golden candlesticks, and in the midst of the candlesticks, one like unto the Son of Man.* Then follows a very particular description of the person who appeared, and of the effect which the vision had upon John, who when he *saw him, fell at his feet as dead;* and, says the Apostle, he laid his right hand upon me, saying unto me, fear not; I am the first and the last; I am *he that liveth, and was dead, and behold I am alive for ever more, amen, and have the keys of Death and Hell.* It is plain that it is the Son of God who speaks in the four last verses of this chapter. And it is also plain that he speaks in the eleventh verse, and twice he calls himself the first and the last; why then may not the words of the eighth verse be spoken of him, by the Apostle, as words he heard him speak? It is one person who speaks to John from the beginning of the eleventh verse to the end of the chapter; and he that calls himself Alpha and Omega, the first and the last, is as much intitled to call himself the Almighty, as to claim the attribute of eternity, which he actually does.

But the attribute Almighty is ascribed to Jesus Christ

Chrift, in the fongs of praife which are fung in Heaven by his Church triumphant. The Saints of God are reprefented as ftanding upon a fea of glafs, having in their hands the harps of God; *and they fing the fong of Mofes the fervant of God, and the fong of the Lamb, faying, great and marvellous are thy works, Lord God Almighty; juft and true are thy ways thou king of faints. Who fhall not fear thee O Lord and glorify thy name, for thou only art holy; for all nations fhall come and worfhip before thee, for thy judgments are made manifeft.* *

This is a very fublime and heavenly fong; it contains the high praifes of the Lord God Almighty, whofe works are great and marvellous; and it will be granted, that the faints of God knew perfectly well that it ought not to be fung in praife of any one, but the true and living God. Now it is very evident, that this very fong of praife is addreffed to the Lamb; the victorious Meffiah, the king of faints, and righteous Judge, whofe judgments were then made manifeft. This fong was not fung by the Lamb, but was fung to his glory and his praife; and even in this fenfe it may with propriety be called the fong of the Lamb; as David calls the fong which he fang in the watches of the night, in praife of his God, the fong of God: *The Lord will command his loving kindneffes*

---

* Rev. xv. Chap.

kindnesses in the day time, and by night his song shall be with me, and my prayer unto the God of my life.

The words of this sacred song shew that it is addressed to, and sung in praise of the Lamb, for who is the king of saints, and whose judgments are made manifest? the judgments of the Messiah, the Lamb; for in this book he is described as the victorious captain of our salvation, who has conquered his and our enemies, avenged his saints, and made manifest his power and his judgments. His enemies are represented as making war with the Lamb, but they are defeated, confounded, and destroyed; these, says John, shall make war with the Lamb, and the Lamb shall overcome them, *for he is Lord of Lords, and King of Kings, and they that are with him are called, and chosen, and faithful.* * I shall produce two more passages of Scripture in which the attribute Almighty, is ascribed unto the Son of God. *And I heard the Angel of the waters say, thou art righteous O Lord, which art, and wast, and art to come, because thou hast judged thus: for they have shed the blood of Saints and Prophets, and thou hast given them blood to drink, for they are worthy. And I heard another out of the Altar say, even so, Lord God Almighty, true and righteous are thy judgments.* †

And again, in another place, *We give thee thanks, O*

---

* Rev. xvii. 14. † Rev. xvi. 7.

O, Lord God Almighty, which art, and waſt, and art to come, becauſe thou haſt taken unto thee thy great power and haſt reigned. And the nations were angry, and thy wrath is come, and the time of the dead, that they ſhould be judged, and that thou ſhouldſt give reward unto thy ſervants the prophets, and to the ſaints, and them that fear thy name, ſmall and great, and ſhouldſt deſtroy them that deſtroy the Earth.*

That theſe words are addreſſed to Chriſt, we may be convinced by the following conſiderations: Firſt, Chriſt as King and head of his Church, governs and defends it; pours out his wrath and his judgments on the nations, and ſubdues his enemies by that power which is able to ſubdue all things. Secondly, he that thus reigns as king of his Church, judges the nations, and avenges his people, is the perſon who ſhall finally judge the world in righteouſneſs. He that reigns and judges, and manifeſts his judgments, antcedent to the laſt judgment, is the ſame that ſhall judge the quick and the dead at the laſt day; when he ſhall finally reward his ſervants that have been faithful unto death; unto theſe he will give a crown of life. Now it is the Son who ſhall judge the world in righteouſneſs; he ſhall *ſit upon the throne of his glory, and before him ſhall be gathered all nations.* He that ſhall come in a viſible manner, in glory, and attended by the holy Angels, and ſhall ſit

* Rev. xi. 17, 18.

fit upon the throne of his glory, is the Son; this shall be the glorious appearing of our great God and Saviour Jesus Christ, when he shall come to take vengeance on them that know not God, and that obey not the gospel of our Lord Jesus Christ: these shall be punished with everlasting destruction, from the presence of the Lord, and from the glory of his power, when he shall come to be glorified in his Saints. We have therefore ascertained the Person who is to be judge at the Great Day; it is the same person who now reigns and judges, and has manifested his judgments, and shall make them more and more manifest in the Earth: but this person who is represented in the book of Revelations, as reigning, judging, avenging and rewarding, is called the Almighty God.

If it be said that the Son exercises judgment now, and shall judge at the Great Day, by a commission from the Father; we grant that all judgment is committed to him; *The Father himself judgeth no man, but hath committed all judgment unto the Son, because he is the son of man.* We believe this Scripture as well as any other, and we believe, *that God hath appointed a day in which he will jugde the world in righteousness, by that man whom he hath ordained.* These words ascertain the person who is to judge, and are no objection to our doctrine; they take away no attribute from the Son of God; they do not prove that

he

he is not Almighty, Omnifcient, and the fearcher of hearts; they only relate to him as fuftaining the mediatorial office and character, as fuch he is anointed to be king of his Church, as fuch, all judgment is committed to him, and becaufe he is the Son of man. But in vain is he anointed king, and the Judge of all, if he is not God as well as man: if he is not all-wife, almighty, the fearcher of hearts, he is not able to execute the offices of King and Judge, to him committed as mediator. We fhall have occafion to fpeak of Chrift as mediator, in a fubfequent difcourfe, and will conclude this fermon with a fhort recapitulation. It is hoped that every unprejudiced reader, has received fatisfactory evidence, that the attributes of Eternity, Omniprefence, and Omnipotence, are afcribed to the fon of God. The Scriptures affure us that he is the Creator of all things; the upholder of all things; and that he is able even to fubdue all things to himfelf. We have feen it revealed in the word of God, that he is the Alpha and Omega, the firft and the laft; that he is the King of Kings and Lord of Lords; the victorious Captain of our Salvation; the Heart-fearching Judge of the quick and of the dead, who will give unto every one according to his works. *O may we be found of him in peace, without fpot, and blamelefs;* may we be *looking for, and hafting unto the coming of the day of God.* Let us take hold of his ftrength, and of his holy covenant; let us fubmit to his authority, and *kifs the Son left he be angry,* and we

we

we *perish from the way, when his wrath is kindled but a little; blessed are all they that put their trust in him.*

SERMON SECOND.

John, 20th Chap. 28th Verse.

And Thomas answered and said unto him, my Lord, and my God.

IN this discourse, it is proposed to shew, that the Divine attributes of Holiness, Justice Mercy, Truth, and Faithfulness, are ascribed to Jesus Christ the son of God.

Secondly, we shall shew that he is called by the divine, adorable, and incommunicable name, Jehovah.

Thirdly, we will quote and illustrate some passages of Scripture, in which Jesus Christ is expresly called God.

The divine attribute of holiness, that is, infinite holiness, comes first under our consideration. The holiness

holiness of God is infinite, he only is holy; he is the Holy One; the Holy One of Jacob; the Holy One of Israel. It cannot be denied, that these words are used to signify an infinite holiness; for God who is infinitely holy, uses these expressions to signify his own holiness; I am, says he, *the Lord your Holy One*. If, then, these words denote the holiness of the living and true God, even the God of Israel, and if the Holy Spirit speaks of the holiness of the Son Christ Jesus, in the same words, and in the same stile, this conclusion, namely, that his holiness is infinite, must evidently follow.

First, then, the Son of God is called, *the Holy One of Israel*; and the Church is encouraged to trust in him as her Creator, her Husband, and her Redeemer: *Thy Maker is thine Husband, the Lord of Hosts is his name; and thy Redeemer the Holy One of Israel; the God of the whole Earth shall he be called.** It is very plain, that these words relate to the Son of God; for he is the husband and the Redeemer of the Church; he is the Bridegroom, and the Church is his Bride, his beloved, his espoused. Jesus, who paid the price of our Redemption, redeemed us to God by his blood, and purchased the Church with his own blood, is the Redeemer, *in whom we have Redemption through his blood, even the forgiveness of sins*. I know, said holy Job, *that my*

---

* Isaiah, liv. 5.

my Redeemer liveth; and that he shall stand at the latter day upon the Earth. But is it necessary to prove what has been acknowledged by the Church of Christ, in all ages of the world, and is testified by the Holy Spirit? Is it necessary to prove that Jesus Christ is the Redeemer? and if it is true that he is the Redeemer, then it is as true, that he is the Holy One of Israel. We might rest the proof of the Son's infinite holiness upon these words alone; for the Holy One of Israel is infinitely holy, and unto him the Church in Heaven, singing the Redeemer's praises, says, *thou only art holy.* *

But again, Jesus Christ is called the *Holy One of God;* and the Psalmist speaking of him, says, thou wilt not suffer *thine Holy One* to see corruption. Jesus is holy as to his Human nature, the holy child Jesus; holy in his miraculous conception, holy in his birth, holy in his life, and holy in his death; but there is an infinite holiness ascribed to him, in the following words of the inspired Prophet: Seventy weeks, says the Prophet Daniel, are determined upon thy people, and upon the holy city, to finish the transgression, and to make an end of sins, and to make reconciliation for iniquity, and to bring in everlasting righteousness, and to seal up the vision, and prophecy, and to anoint *the Most Holy.* † Now this title, the Most Holy, is not
ascribed

---

* Rev. xv. 4. † Daniel ix. 24.

ascribed to Christ, in a relative or comparative sense, to signify that he was more holy than any other man; or upon a comparison, the most holy of all men; this would be too low a character for the blessed Jesus, the Lamb of God, who was holy, harmless, undefiled and separate from sinners. To say in a relative or comparative sense, that Jesus surpassed in holiness, the holiest saint that ever lived, is only to say that Jesus was more holy than sinful dust and ashes; far be it from us to say that this was the meaning of the inspired Prophet. If then these words, the most holy, cannot be taken in the comparative sense above-mentioned; if to say that Jesus was the most holy of all men, using the superlative degree of comparison, is not sufficient to express his sinless and untainted holiness as man; then they must be understood in an absolute or positive sense, to signify his perfect holiness as man, without any relative view to the holiness of other men.* But in this sense they cannot be used; because, in this sense, they are too high to express the perfect holiness of Jesus as man, as in the former sense they are too low and insufficient; for the holiness of which human nature in its perfection is capable, cannot entitle a man to the glorious character of, the most holy. The Divine nature alone is most holy; the holiness of this nature is eternal, underived, infinite.

In

* If Jesus is no more than a man.

In the temple of God, there was an holy place where the tribes of Israel worshipped, and offered their sacrifices: and there was another place, called the Most Holy; here, the sacred memorials of God's special favour and love to his people, were deposited and preserved; in this most holy place was the mercy seat, and above this seat, between the spreading wings of the Cherubim, there was a visible appearance of the glory of God, a symbol of the special presence of the Holy One of Israel, in his holy place. One would think that there could not be a more glorious Temple than that which was built by king Solomon, at an immense expense, ornamented and furnished with more than royal magnificence; and above all dedicated to the living and true God, whose glory at the dedication, filled the house. Could any temple be more glorious than this, in which the glory of God appeared, and which he hallowed unto himself; to put, says he, *my name there for ever, and mine eyes and mine heart shall be there perpetually?* Yes, after this Temple was destroyed as God declared it should be, in case of Irael's apostacy, I say after the destruction of this house, God promised to make the glory of the latter house, greater than the glory of the former; and he performed his promise. *Thus saith the Lord of Hosts, yet once, it is a little while, and I will shake the Heavens and the Earth, and the Sea and the*

the dry land; and I will shake all nations, and the desire of all nations shall come, and I will fill this house with glory, saith Lord of Hosts. The glory of this latter house shall be greater than of the former, saith the Lord of Hosts; and in this place will I give peace, saith the Lord of Hosts.* And again, saith the Lord, by the Prophet Malachi, *the Lord whom ye seek, shall suddenly come to his Temple, even the messenger of the covenant whom ye delight in.* All these things have been accomplished, according to the word of the Lord; the Lord did terribly shake the Earth; and when he had turned wars into peace, the Prince of Peace was born: The desire of all nations came in the fulness of time; the Lord, the Angel of the Covenant, whose coming was anxiously expected, more especially by those that were looking for the salvation of God, came suddenly to his Temple, and there preached the glad tidings of the Gospel, proclaimed his peace, and gave unto his disciples that peace which the world could not give. The presence of the Messiah was the glory of the latter house; and the glory of the latter house was greater than the glory of the former. And why was it greater? Because the glory of the former house, was only a luminous symbol of the special presence of the Holy One of Israel; but in the latter house, the glory of the Holy One was seen in the

---

* Haggai ii. 5, 9.

the perfon of the great IMMANUEL, which is, being interpreted, *God with us.* In the latter houfe God appeared manifeft in the flefh ; *God was manifeft in the flefh,* fays the Apoftle; and, fays the Evangelifts, *the word was made flefh, and dwelt among us, and we beheld his glory, the glory as of the only begotten of the Father, full of grace and truth.*

It would not be difficult to fhew, were it neceffary at prefent, that he who manifefted himfelf to the Church in the wildernefs, and chofe a dwelling-place in the fanctuary of the Tabernacle, and afterwards in the holy place of Solomon's Temple, was the Son of God ; even the fame perfon who is called the Angel of the Covenant, and who appeared incarnate in the latter Temple. But upon the fuppofition that it was the Father who appeared, in a bright fymbol of his fpecial or extraordinary prefence, between the wings of the Cherubim in the fanctuary of the tabernacle, and of Solomon's temple ; and that it was the Son who appeared in the latter temple, and not in the former ; yet it muft follow as a juft conclufion, that the holinefs of the Son is not inferior to the holinefs of the Father; becaufe, the prefence of the Son of God, could not have made the glory of the latter houfe greater than the glory of the former, if his holinefs was inferior to the holinefs of Him who was the glory of the former houfe.

The

The evangelical Prophet saw in a vision, the glory of the Son of God; and he heard the Seraphim ascribing to him the Divine attribute of holiness. The words of the Prophet are worthy of our most serious consideration; I saw, says Isaiah, the Lord sitting upon a throne high and lifted up, and his train filled the Temple. Above it stood the Seraphim, each one had six wings, with twain he covered his face, and with twain he covered his feet, and with twain he did fly. *And one cried unto another and said, Holy, Holy, Holy, is the Lord of Hosts, the whole earth is full of his glory. And the posts of the door moved at the voice of him that cried, and the house was filled with smoke. Then said I, woe is me for I am undone, because I am a man of unclean lips; for mine eyes have seen the King, the Lord of Hosts.** This glory which Isaiah saw, was the glory of the Son, he is called the Lord of Hosts, in his presence the Seraphim cover their faces with their wings, and unto him they ascribe the glory of his holiness, saying, Holy, Holy, Holy, is the Lord of Hosts, the whole earth is full of his glory. That these words relate to the Son of God, and that the Prophet saw his glory, is asserted by the Evangelist John, who could not mistake the Prophet's meaning, nor misapply his words; *These things,* said Esaias, *when he saw his glory and spake of him*†.

We

---

* Isaiah vi. 1, 5. John xii. 41.

We may now proceed to shew, that the divine attributes, Justice, Mercy, Truth, and Faithfulness, are ascribed to Jesus Christ the Son of God. These attributes are ascribed to him in the highest sense of the words, in the same stile and language that the inspired writers use to express these attributes and perfections of the living and true God. The Psalmist, singing the high praises of his God, uses these remarkable words; *Justice and Judgment are the habitation of thy throne, mercy accompanied with truth shall go before thy face.* This is a very sublime and beautiful passage; Justice and Judgment are represented as a sacred temple where the throne of God is fixed upon immovable foundations; and where, God who is infinitely righteous delights to dwell. And words of the same import, and expressive of equal dignity, are addressed to the Son; thus, for instance, *Thy throne, O God, is for ever and ever, a sceptre of righteousness is the sceptre of thy kingdom.* And, says the Prophet,, *with righteousness shall he judge the poor, and reprove with equity, for the meek of the earth; and he shall smite the earth with the rod of his mouth, and with the breath of his lips shall he slay the wicked. And righteousness shall be the girdle of his loins, and faithfulness the girdle of his reins* *. Jesus is called the *Just one, the sun of righteousness, and everlasting righteousness.* Jesus is the judge of all the earth; and shall not the judge of all the earth do right?

* Isaiah xi. 5, 6.

Must not his justice be infinite? The judge of angels and men, the judge of the quick and of the dead, the heart-searching judge, who must be omniscient because he is the searcher of hearts; must be infinitely just, to give unto every one according to his ways. Jesus is called, *The Lord, the righteous Judge;* and before his tribunal we must all appear; *We shall all stand before the judgment seat of Christ; for as it is written, saith the Lord, every knee shall bow to me, and every tongue shall confess to God. So then every one of us shall give an account of himself to God**. Here, the Judge before whose judgment seat we shall all stand, is called God; and on the great and terrible day of the Lord, his righteousness shall be acknowledged to be infinite, both by his saints and his enemies: Elements melting with fervent heat! the Heavens rolling together as a scroll! Angels applauding! Saints Triumphant! shall declare the righteousness of the Almighty, all-wise, and infinitely righteous Judge.

As our God is just and righteous, so also is he merciful; his mercy is infinite; his mercy is everlasting; his mercy endureth for ever; his mercy is great unto the Heavens. *Who is a God like unto thee that pardoneth iniquity, and passeth by the transgression of the remnant of his heritage? He retaineth not his anger for ever, because he delighteth in mercy.*
Thus

---

* Rom. xiv. 11, 12.

Thus the mercy of God is illustriously displayed, in the forgiveness of sins, and in sending his own Son to be the propitiation for our sins: And the mercy of Jesus the Son of God, is illustriously manifested by his redeeming love, and his pity and compassion to poor sinners. If Lot said unto God, thou hast magnified thy mercy in saving my life; how has the Son of God magnified his mercy, in saving our souls from everlasting death! How has he magnified his mercy, in his divine condescension, in becoming poor for our sakes, that we through his poverty might be made rich! He hath glorified his grace in dying for us, the just for the unjust, that he might bring us to God. View the mercy of the blessed Jesus, in his condescension, in his humiliation, in his life, sufferings, agony and bitter passion, and confess that the love of Jesus passeth knowledge, is unsearchable and divine. Jesus is praised in heaven, for his mercy, and for the wonderful works of his grace; but he could not be praised for his redeeming grace and love, if his grace and love are not divine perfections, that is, if his mercy is not infinite; because, he only whose mercy is infinite, is to be adored and praised for the exercise of mercy. Farther, the mercy of the Redeemer is spoken of as divine mercy, even the mercy of God, when it is said; *for a small moment have I forsaken thee, but with great mercies will I gather thee; in a little wrath I hid my face from thee, but with everlasting kindness*

ness will I have mercy on thee, saith the Lord thy Redeemer. This everlasting kindness, with which the Redeemer will have mercy on his Church, is the kindness of that God, whose mercy endureth for ever. The Apostle Paul speaks of the mercy of Christ, as the mercy of God, when he says, *I obtained mercy of the Lord to be faithful;* and, as the mercy of that God who is long-suffering and slow to anger, when he says, *I thank Jesus Christ our Lord, who hath enabled me, for that he counted me faithful, putting me into the ministry; who was before, a blasphemer, and a persecutor, and injurious; but I obtained mercy, because I did it ignorantly, in unbelief. And the grace of our Lord Jesus was exceeding abundant, with faith, and love which is in Christ Jesus. This is a faithful saying, and worthy of all acceptation, that Christ Jesus came into the world to save sinners; of whom I am chief. Howbeit, for this cause I obtained mercy, that in me first, Jesus Christ might shew forth all long-suffering, for a pattern to them which should hereafter believe on him to life everlasting* *. In these words, the Apostle acknowledges the pardoning mercy of Jesus; he acknowledges his long-suffering patience; he calls it *all long-suffering;* now, that mercy which pardoneth sinners; that mercy which we are commanded to look for *unto eternal life;* † that mercy which is long-suffering, and that long suffering which

---

* 1. Tim. i. 14, 15, 16. † Jude 21st ver.

which is Salvation, muſt be infinite. The truth and faithfulneſs of Jeſus, are ſpoken of in the Scriptures, in the moſt exalted terms; He is the *truth and the life; the true God and eternal life;* his name is *Faithful and True*. The Diſciples encouraged each other by the truth and faithfulneſs of Chriſt, they believed in him, and truſted in him for the accompliſhment of his promiſes; they looked unto him for promiſed protection and deliverance, and they confided in his truth and faithfulneſs. *The Lord is faithful*, ſays the Apoſtle, *who ſhall eſtabliſh you and keep you from evil*. Chriſtians believe in Jeſus, and depend upon his truth and faithfulneſs, with that divine faith and hope, with which the ancient worthies depended upon the God of truth and faithfulneſs; nor have Chriſtians any reaſon to be aſhamed of their hope, it is an hope that maketh not aſhamed. The Apoſtle rejoiced in hope, though in bonds; his chain ſat light upon him, becauſe he could ſay, *for the hope of Iſrael am I bound with this chain*. The Pſalmiſt, ſpeaking of the Son of God, pronounces a bleſſing upon all thoſe *that hope in him*. It is unlawful to place religious hope and confidence in one whoſe truth and faithfulneſs are not divine, that is, infinite. It is our duty to truſt in God, and to hope in God, and in none but him; in thee, O Lord, do I hope, ſaith the Pſalmiſt, and again, *thou art my hope, O, Lord God, thou art my truſt from my youth*. God is called the *God of hope*,

G and

and Jesus Christ is called, *the Hope of glory*. He *is Our Hope*, and we are said to have hope in him, not with regard to the things of this world only, but eminently, with regard to the world to come, even the hope of eternal life. *Beloved*, says the Apostle, *now are we the sons of God, and it doth not yet appear what we shall be; but we know that when he*, that is, God the Son, *shall appear, we shall be like him, for we shall see him as he is. And every one that hath this hope in him, purifieth himself, even as he is pure.* * The true and faithful God was the hope of Israel, and Jesus Christ is the hope of glory, and our hope; is he not therefore the true and faithful God? Is it lawful for Christians to hope in Jesus, if he is not the true and faithful God?

' We are next to shew that Jesus Christ the Son of God, is called JEHOVAH. But before we do this, it may be useful to give some account of this name, and its signification. It is the adorable and incommunicable name of the living and true God, and is never ascribed to any but him. It is an essential name, a name of essence, and signifies the Eternal, necessary, underived existence of that Being who is self-existent; and which is, and was, and is to come. The name, JEHOVAH, says a judicious critic, † " sets out God's eternity, in that it contains all times, future, present, and past; " thus,

says

---

* 1. John iii. 2, 4.   † Leigh's Critca Sacra.

says he, "this title given to Christ, which is, and which was, and which is to come, is an express interpretation of JEHOVAH." This name is derived from a verb which signifies to BE, and denotes the eternal existence of that God, from whom all other beings have received their existence, and in whom we live, and move, and have our being. This name is of the same signification with I AM, and I AM THAT I AM; as we may learn from what God said to Moses, when he sent him to the children of Israel in Egypt. On this occasion the Lord proclaimed his great and glorious name; *and God said unto Moses, I AM THAT I AM; and he said, thus shalt thou say unto the children of Israel, I AM hath sent me unto you. And God said moreover unto Moses, thus shalt thou say unto the children of Israel, the Lord God of your fathers* (the word here translated Lord, is JEHOVAH) *the God of Abraham, the God of Isaac, and the God of Jacob hath sent me unto you; this is my name for ever, and this is my memorial unto all generations.* * To shew that this name is peculiar to God, that it is his name, and that it is incommunicable; we shall quote two passages of Scripture which are clear and decisive: *I am the Lord, that is my name, and my glory will I not give unto another, neither my praise unto graven Images.* † The word, Lord, is in the original, JEHOVAH. And says

---

* Exod. iii. 14, 15.   † Isaiah xlii. 8.

says the Psalmist, *Thou whose name alone is* JEHOVAH, *art the most high over all the earth.* *

Now to shew that Jesus Christ the son of God, is called by this divine, adorable, and incommunicable name of God; it will be sufficient to quote a few texts of scripture, such as most clearly and directly prove the point in question. We shall first consider that remarkable prophecy of Isaiah, respecting John the Baptist, the fore-runner of the Messiah, and the person who prepared his way before him. The Prophet calls the Baptist, *the voice of him that crieth in the wilderness, prepare ye the way of the Lord,* JEHOVAH, *make straight in the desert, a way for our God.* There can be no doubt in this matter; for John the Baptist is constantly spoken of in the Gospels, as this voice, and as the fore-runner of the Messiah. John confessed that he was not the Messiah; nor that light, nor that Prophet; he knew his office and his place, and spoke of himself and his baptism, as nothing in comparison of Christ and his baptism: *I indeed,* says John, *baptize you with water, unto repentance, but he that cometh after me is mightier than I, whose shoes I am not worthy to bear; he shall baptize you with the Holy Ghost and with fire. Whose fan is in his hand, and he will throughly purge his floor, and gather his wheat into his garner; but he will burn the chaff with unquenchable*

* lxxxiii. Psalm.

able fire. * Let us hear John's record and confession, *and this is the record of John, when the Jews sent priests and Levites from Jerusalem to ask him, who art thou? and he confessed and denied not, but confessed, I am not the Christ.* And after answering several questions in the negative, he told them who he was, *he said I am the voice of one crying in the wilderness, make straight the way of the Lord, as said the prophet Esaias.* † Let us also hear what Zacharias said of his son when he was born; *thou child, shalt be called the prophet of the Highest, for thou shalt go before the face of the Lord to prepare his ways.* And says the Evangelist, *the same came for a witness to bear witness of the light, that all men through him might believe.* The only thing here necessary to be ascertained, is, that John the Baptist prepared the way of Christ, as his fore-runner; and this is sufficiently done by what has been said, and by the Evangelist Mark, at the beginning of his Gospel, where speaking of the Baptist, he says, *as it is written in the Prophets, behold I send my messenger before thy face, which shall prepare thy way before thee. The voice of one crying in the wilderness, prepare ye the way of the Lord, make his paths straight.*

Again, the prophet Jeremiah calls the Son of God, JEHOVAH, in the following words: Behold the days come, saith the Lord, that I will raise unto David a righteous

---

* Matth. iii. 11, 12.   † John i. 23.

a righteous Branch; and a King shall reign and prosper, and shall execute judgment and justice in the earth. In his days Judah shall be saved, and Israel shall dwell safely; and this is HIS name, whereby HE shall be called, THE LORD OUR RIGHTEOUSNESS; that is, JEHOVAH OUR RIGHTEOUSNESS.* Another Prophet, under the influence of the same spirit, calls the Saviour, JEHOVAH, in these words; *surely shall one say, in the Lord,* that is, JEHOVAH, *have I righteousness and strength; even to him shall men come, and all that are incensed against him, shall be ashamed: In the Lord shall all the seed of Israel be justified and shall glory.* It is very evident that these prophecies relate to the Messiah; he is our righteousness, it is he *who of God is made unto us, wisdom, and righteousness, and sanctification, and redemption; that according as it is written, he that glorieth, let him glory in the Lord.* † It is by the Lord Jesus Christ that we are justified, for, says the Apostle, *be it known unto you therefore, men and brethren, that through this man, is preached unto you the forgiveness of sins; and by him, all that believe are justified from all things, from which ye could not be justified by the law of Moses. Beware therefore, lest that come upon you which is spoken of in the prophets, behold ye despisers, and wonder, and perish; for I work a work in your*

days,

---

* Jer. xxiii. 5, 6. † Cor. i. 30, 31.

days, a work which you shall in no wise believe, though a man declare it unto you. * In that remarkable passage of Isaiah's prophecy, formerly quoted, and which the Evangelist applies to the Son of God, he is called JEHOVAH TSEBAOTH; *Holy, Holy, Holy, is the Lord of Hosts, the whole earth is full of his glory. Wo is me,* said the Prophet, *for I am undone, because I am a man of unclean lips, for mine eyes have seen the King, the Lord of Hosts.*

There is another prediction of the same Prophet, which evidently relates to the Messiah, and in which he is called JEHOVAH; the words are these; *sanctify the Lord of Hosts himself, and let him be your fear, and let him be your dread; and he shall be for a sanctuary; but for a stone of stumbling, and for a rock of offence to both houses of Israel, for a gin and a snare to the inhabitants of Jerusalem. And many among them shall stumble and fall and be broken, and be snared and taken.* † How exactly was this prediction fulfilled; at the coming of the Messiah! He was a sanctuary to them that sanctified him in their hearts; he was a city of refuge to all that believed in him; but he was a stone of stumbling and a rock of offence to the unbelieving Jews; and in their miserable destruction, was the latter part of this prophecy most awfully accomplished. I shall conclude this head of discourse with one quotation more; the prophet Zechariah,

after

---

* Acts xiii. 38, 40. † Isaiah viii. 13, 14.

after having denounced the judgments of God, upon the inhabitants of the land of Judea, mentions the very price for which the Messiah should be sold and betrayed: But he that was sold and betrayed into the hands of sinners, is that very Lord who spake by the mouth of his Prophet, saying, *if ye think good, give me my price; and if not, forbear: so they weighed for my price thirty pieces of silver. And the Lord,* JEHOVAH, *said unto me, cast it unto the potter, a goodly price that I was prised at of them.* *

We presume it has been proved, that the Lord Jesus Christ, is called by the divine, and incommunicable name, JEHOVAH, this is the name of God, his name alone is JEHOVAH; *the Lord he is God, there is none else. Who is God save the Lord? Hear O, Israel, the Lord our God is one Lord.* That the Father is JEHOVAH, will not be denied; that the Son is JEHOVAH, has been proved; and that the Holy Ghost is JEHOVAH, can be proved by the same kind of arguments, namely, express declarations of the holy Scriptures: † These Three, therefore, are one JEHOVAH, one, in a divine and incomprehensible unity of an incomprehensible essence.

We

---

* Zach. xi, 12, 13.

† That the Holy Ghost is JEHOVAH, is plain from a passage in the prophecy of Ezekiel, where the Prophet says, the Spirit lifted me up and took me away, and I went in bitterness

We come now to the third and laſt head of this diſ‑ courſe; and ſhall conclude this Sermon with ſome quotations of Scripture, in which, Jeſus Chriſt is expreſsly called God.

Let us then begin with the words of the evange‑ lical Prophet, who, ſpeaking of the Meſſiah, expreſſes himſelf in the following words; *behold, your God will come with vengeance, even God with a recompence, he will come and ſave you.* But ſome might aſk, when will our God come? we have been long looking for his appearance, and waiting for his ſalvation;

neſs in the heat of my ſpirit; but the hand of the Lord, in the original, JEHOVAH, was ſtrong upon me. The Holy Ghoſt is called *the Eternal Spirit*, the Omnipreſent Spirit; *where ſhall I go from thy ſpirit? or whither ſhall I fly from thy preſence? The Spirit ſearcheth all things; yea the deep things of God.* He is *the Spirit of wiſdom.* He is the Cre‑ ator, for Job ſays, *the Spirit of God hath made me;* and again, it is written, *Thou ſendeſt forth thy ſpirit and they are created.* The Holy Ghoſt is called God, for ſays the Apoſtle to Ananias, *why hath Satan filled thine heart to lie unto the Holy Ghoſt? thou haſt not lied unto man, but unto God.* And again, *how is it that ye have agreed together to tempt the ſpirit of the Lord?* There is a ſin, more immedi‑ ately committed againſt this Holy one, which is called the unpardonable ſin; *whoſoever ſpeaketh againſt the Holy Ghoſt, it ſhall not be forgiven him, neither in this world, nor in that which is to come.* I have juſt mentioned theſe particulars, reſpecting the divinity of the Holy Ghoſt, and refer the reader to the Holy Scriptures for further information.

H

salvation; when will he come to avenge and save his people? The Prophet indeed does not tell the precise time, but he shews the signs of his coming; and he gives certain tokens whereby the people might know their God, when he should come: And these, says the Prophet, are the signs of his coming, *the eyes of the blind shall be opened, and the ears of the deaf shall be unstopped, then shall the lame man leap as an Hart, and the tongue of the dumb sing. For in the wilderness shall waters break out, and streams in the desert.* * These predictions were accomplished when the Messiah came, and entered upon his public ministry; he opened the eyes of the blind, unstopped the ears of the deaf, made the lame to walk, and the tongue of the dumb to sing; Jesus applied this prophecy to himself, and appealed to these signs, even his own wonderful works, as infallible evidences that he was the true Messiah. When John the Baptist sent two of his disciples unto Jesus, with this question, art thou he that should come, or do we look for another? our Lord answered, by applying the words of the Prophet to himself, and shewing that in him they were fulfilled; go, says he, *and shew John again those things which ye do hear and see: the blind receive their sight, and the lame walk, the lepers are cleansed and the deaf hear, the dead are raised up, and the poor have the Gospel preached*

* Isaiah xxxv. 4, 5, 6.

ed unto them, and blessed is he whosoever shall not be offended in me. *

The prophet Isaiah, calls Jesus the mighty God; and one would think that this is sufficient to prove the Divinity of Jesus Christ; if he is the mighty God, then surely he is really and truly God. It has been proved, in a former discourse, that he is Almighty, the Creator of all things, and able even to subdue all things to himself; is it not, therefore, irrational to say that Jesus is God, but not equal to the Almighty Creator of all things? Is it not absurd to say that he is God, and yet to deny that he is all-perfect? In God there is not, there cannot be any imperfection; there is not a superior and an inferior God.

When Jesus is called IMMANUEL, he is called God, even God with us; the Word was made flesh and dwelt among us; and we know that he who is called the Word, is the Son of God. This is he who took upon him the form of a servant; this is he that took on him the seed of Abraham; this is he that descended from the Fathers of the Jewish nation, as concerning the flesh, *who is over all God blessed for ever.* In Jesus *dwelleth all the fulness of the Godhead bodily;* the beloved Disciple calls him the true God and eternal life; and, the Apostle Paul, speaking of the Incarnation of the Son of God, says,

and

* Matthew xi. 4, 6.

and without controversy, great is the mystery of Godliness; God was manifest in the flesh. The Apostle, exhorting the Elders of the Church at Ephesus, uses these emphatical words, feed the Church of God, which he hath purchased with his own blood: But these words must be something more than mysterious, if he who shed his blood for the redemption of his Church, was not God and man in one person; but of this more hereafter. Again, Christians are exhorted to adorn the doctrine of God our Saviour in all things; for the grace of God that bringeth salvation hath appeared unto all men, teaching us, that denying ungodliness and worldly lusts, we should live soberly, righteously, and godly in this present world; *Looking for that blessed hope, and the glorious appearing of the great God, and our Saviour Jesus Christ;* * *who gave himself for us, that he might redeem us from all iniquity, and purify unto himself a peculiar people zealous of good works.* Here, the Lord Jesus Christ is called God, yea, the great God and Saviour, as will clearly appear from the following considerations. First, the construction of the words in the original, shews us, that the Apostle speaks only of one person, namely, the Redeemer who gave himself for us, who is ascended up into Heaven, and who will appear the second time, without sin unto salvation; and whose glorious appearing, Christians look for with

* Titus ii. 13.

with hope and expectation. The word, ἐπιφανεια, which is translated, appearing, in all other passages where it occurs, relates to Jesus Christ; once, it relates to his first coming, in every other instance, it relates to his second coming, when he shall appear in a very glorious manner, to judge the world in righteousness. He shall come, and shall be seen coming in the clouds of Heaven, with power and great glory: *Behold he cometh with clouds, and every eye shall see him, and they also which pierced him.* And if this is the sense in which the word is used, except where it relates to the first coming of Christ, why should we not understand it in this sense here? Christ shall come in his own glory, and in his Father's, and of the Holy Angels; and let this glory be what it may, it is plain that it is the Son, and not the Father, who shall come, appear, and be seen by every eye. But a literal translation of the whole text, will set the matter in a clear light; and the following translation is not only literal, but the exact order of the words in the original is preserved, viz. "Looking for the blessed hope, and the illustrious appearing of the glory of the great God and Saviour of us, Jesus Christ." The words may be translated with a sufficient degree of literal exactness, and more conformable to the idiom of our language, as follows: "Looking for the blessed hope, and the illustrious appearance of the glory

glory of our great God and Saviour Jesus Christ." Some are of opinion that the word, *and*, should be taken exegetically, and translated, *even*, so that the text would be read thus, "Looking for that blessed hope and the glorious appearing of the great God, *even*, our Saviour Jesus Christ." But the second translation which I have offered, is sufficient to prove our point; and for the justness of it, I appeal to the marginal translation of the first verse of the second epistle of Peter; the words are, Simon Peter, a servant and an Apostle of Jesus Christ, to them that have obtained like precious faith with us, *through the righteousness* * *of God, and our Saviour Jesus Christ*: This latter clause should be translated, " through the righteousness of our God and Saviour Jesus Christ;" which our excellent translators have accordingly done in the margin. Now this passage, and that in the epistle to Titus, are of the same grammatical construction, except, the order of one word, ʼημων, that is *our* should be considered as making a difference of grammatical construction, which I think it cannot; but if it makes any difference, it appears to be in favour of our doctrine. I think it unnecessary to shew the justness of the marginal translation, of the first verse of the second epistle of Peter, it is only

a matter

---

* *Through the Righteousness*, would be better translated "in the Righteousness."

a matter of surprise, that the Translators did not put it in the text; if the last verse of this epistle is justly translated, viz. *Grow in grace, and in the knowledge of our Lord, and Saviour Jesus Christ*, then the marginal translation of the first verse is just, because the grammatical construction of both is the same.

It cannot be denied that Jesus Christ is called God; I have quoted several texts of Scripture in which he is so called; and many more might be mentioned, were it necessary. The words of my text are clear and decisive, for there the Apostle calls Jesus his Lord and his God; but it is of great importance to ascertain in what sense, Jesus Christ is so called. He is called God, in the strict and proper sense of the word; and this we will now endeavour to prove. First, we are always to understand every word and every sentence, both in the sacred scriptures, and in all other writings, in a literal, strict, and proper sense, except necessity obliges us to take them figuratively; that is, except the words appear to be figurative, or cannot be taken in a strict literal sense without absurdity. When Idols are called Gods, it is easy to see in what sense they are so called: they were so called by their deluded worshippers; but the inspired writers declare that they are lying vanities, dumb idols and an abomination; and sometimes, they are called gods, in derision. They are entirely out of the question. But are not men sometimes called Gods? we grant that they are; but when they are so called, there is always some mark, by which we may perceive in what sense; there is always something said to shew that the word must be taken figuratively. Thus when the Lord says unto Moses, I have made thee a God to Pharaoh, we must understand these words, as relating to the mission which Moses received from God, the authority he was invested with, or in other words, that he was in God's stead, the minister of God; no one can believe that Moses was really and truly God. When persons in high office, and exercising high power are called Gods, it is from some faint resemblance of the power and authority of God over his subjects; but it is said, *God judgeth among the gods,* and again, *I have said ye are gods, and all of you are children of the Most High, but ye shall die like men.* There is nothing easier than to distinguish the true God, from those who are only called gods in a figurative sense; but in what sense is he called God, unto whom the divine attributes are ascribed! there is no absurdity in calling him God, in the strict and proper sense of the word, who is possessed of the divine perfections, and consequently, of that nature to which these perfections belong. If it has been proved that any one divine attribute is ascribed to Jesus Christ, if it has been proved that

he

he is *Jehovah*, if it has been proved that he is *our God and Saviour*, then he is really and truly God; for the true God, and, he only, can be called *our God*. In what sense is he called God, who is eternal, unchangeable, omnipresent, omniscient, and almighty? in what sense is he called God, who is most holy, whose mercy we look for unto eternal life, whose long-suffering is salvation, whose grace is sufficient for his people, whose strength is perfected in their weakness, who is able to save even to the uttermost, and who is himself, the Lord of hosts, and the Lord our righteousness? in what sense is he called God, who is our great God and Saviour, the Prince of life, the Lord of glory, the Lord of Lords and King of Kings? He that is the Lord of Lords, is the Lord of glory; he that is the King of Kings, is the King of glory; and who is the King of glory? *The Lord strong and mighty, The Lord strong and mighty in battle. Lift up your heads, O ye gates, even lift them up ye everlasting doors, and the King of glory shall come in.* Who is this King of glory? the Lord of hosts, he is the King of glory. In what sense is he called God, who is the heart searching judge of the quick and of the dead, who shall judge the world in righteousness, and give unto every one according to his ways? Lastly, in what sense is he called God, in whom dwelleth all the fulness of the God-head bodily, who is in the Father, and the Father in him, and who says I

and

and my Father are one. Philip said unto Jesus shew us the Father; let the answer of our Lord be forever recorded: *have I been so long time with you, and yet thou hast not known me, Philip? he that hath seen me hath seen the Father; and how sayest thou then, shew us the Father? believest thou not that I am in the Father and the Father in me?* Jesus is the brightness of the Father's glory, and the express image of his person. And the everlasting Father declares that his Son is his equal, saying, *awake, O sword, against my shepherd, and smite the man that is my fellow saith the Lord of Hosts.* God hath commanded the Angels to worship the Son; and men are commanded to *honour the Son even as they honour the Father.* Let us neither contradict the word, nor disobey the commandment of our God; but let us ascribe glory, and honour, and blessing, and praise, unto the Father, Son, and Holy Ghost, now, and for ever, Amen.

SERMON THIRD.

John, 20th Chap. 28th Verse.

And Thomas answered and said unto him, my Lord and my God.

IN the following discourse, we will endeavour to prove that Jesus Christ is the object of adoration and religious worship.

It is recorded in the old Testament, that the Patriarch Jacob addressed his prayer to the Son of God; and that he implored his blessing upon his children, saying, *the Angel which redeemed me from all evil, bless the lads* *. Who is this redeeming Angel, this Angel who can redeem from *all evil?* the answer

* Genesis xlviii. 15, 16.

answer is obvious; this Angel is the Angel of the covenant, the great Redeemer, who can redeem the souls of his people, and *who gave himself for us, that he might redeem us from all iniquity.* He that redeems us from all evil, must redeem from sin, must be able to save to the uttermost, must be able not only to grant temporal deliverances to his people, but also to grant deliverance from the guilt and dominion of sin, which in its nature and consequences, is the greatest of all evils. This redeeming Angel is not a created Angel, he is the creator of Angels, the creator of all things, visible, and invisible. The Angel unto whom Jacob prayed, is called the God of Abraham, Isaac, and Jacob, the God before whom Abraham and Isaac did walk, the God who fed Jacob all his life long, unto that very day on which Jacob addressed this prayer unto him. This Angel is the hearer of prayer, is able to confer blessings, and is praised in Heaven for his redeeming love; *worthy art thou to take the book, and to open the seals thereof; for thou wast slain, and hast redeemed us unto God by thy blood. Worthy is the Lamb that was slain, to receive power, and riches, and wisdom, and strength, and honour, and glory, and blessing* *. The Patriarchs were not ignorant of the Redeemer, nor of that redemption that is in him. Abraham saw his day, and rejoiced; and he believed the promise, that in his seed, all nations of the earth

---

* Rev. v. 9, 12.

earth should be blessed. This redeemer was promised to our first parents, when it was said, that the seed of the woman should bruise the head of the serpent. Job knew his redeemer; *I know, says he, that my redeemer liveth; and that he shall stand at the latter day upon the earth. And though after my skin, worms destroy this body, yet in my flesh shall I see God; whom I shall see for myself, and mine eyes shall behold and not another; though my reins be consumed within me**.

The same person, even the Son of God, was worshipped by Joshua, when he appeared unto him as the Captain of the Lord's host, in the likeness of a man, having a drawn sword in his hand; *Joshua fell on his face to the earth, and did worship; and said unto him, what saith my Lord unto his servant? and the Captain of the Lord's host said unto Joshua, loose thy shoe from off thy foot: for the place where thou standest is holy* †. That Jesus Christ our Saviour is the Captain of the Lord's host, we have very convincing evidence; he is called *the Captain of our salvation,* and in the book of the revelation, he is spoken of, as the Captain, the leader of the heavenly armies. John saw the Heavens opened, and he saw the great Messiah; he saw his Vesture dipt in blood, and he knew him to be the Word of God: He saw him at the head of the Heavenly armies, for he informs us that

* Job. xix. 25. 27. † Joshua v. 14. 15.

that *the armies which were in Heaven followed him.* If the Son of God is the Captain of the Lord's host, then he is the person whom Joshua worshipped, falling down on his face to the earth, before the presence of divine Majesty. When God forbids the worshipping of idols, he says, thou shalt not bow down thyself to them nor serve them; and it is as unlawful to bow down to Angels, and to serve them: God alone is the object of religious worship and service. But Joshua fell down on his face, before the Captain of the Lord's host, worshipped him, called him his Lord, acknowledged himself his servant, and at his command, loosed his shoe from off his foot. The captain of the Lord's host appeared to Joshua, to give him his orders for the conducting of a particular expedition: and after having claimed divine honours, proceeds to tells him, that he had delivered Jericho, and the king thereof, and all the mighty men of valour, into his hand. This Captain of the Lord's host is, in the sixth chapter of the book of Joshua, called the Lord, that is, JEHOVAH. But is it worthy of particular notice, that the Captain of the Lord's host claims divine worship, in commanding Joshua to loose his shoe from off his foot, and in giving him this reason why he should do so, namely, *the place where thou standest is holy.* This cannot be considered, but as a declaration on the one part, and an acknowledgment on the other, of the special presence of the holy

holy one of Ifrael; for when the angel of the Lord appeared to Mofes, in the bufh, he commanded him to do the very fame thing, and for the very fame reafon, that the Captain of the Lord's hoft commanded Jofhua to do. There is good ground to believe that the perfon who appeared to Mofes, and who is called Jehovah, and the God of Abraham*, is the very fame perfon who appeared to Jofhua; but granting that thefe were diftinct perfons, they claimed and received the fame divine honours.

The Pfalmift afferts that the Son of God is to be worfhipped when he fays, all kings fhall fall down before him; all nations fhall ferve him: For he fhall deliver the needy when he crieth; the poor alfo, and him that hath no helper. He fhall fpare the poor and needy, and fhall fave the fouls of the needy. He fhall redeem their foul from deceit and violence, and precious fhall their blood be in his fight. And he fhall live, and to him fhall be given of the gold of Sheba; *prayer alfo fhall be made for him continually and daily fhall he be praifed*†. His name fhall endure forever; his name fhall be continued as long as the fun; *and men fhall be bleffed in him; all nations fhall call him bleffed.* It is the conftant prayer of the Church, that the kingdom of Chrift may flourifh and profper; and in this fenfe, prayer may be faid
to

---

* Exodus, iii. chap.   † Pfalm, lxxii.

to be made for him. But if he shall be praised daily if he is the object of daily praise, we may also address our prayers unto him, for praise is a noble part of prayer. We must not praise one whom it is unlawful to pray to, nor pray unto one, whom it is unlawful to address in praise. The Psalmist says unto the church, *Hearken, O daughter, and consider, and incline thine ear; forget also thine own people, and thy father's house. So shall the King greatly desire thy beauty; for he is thy Lord, and worship thou him.*

When Jesus was born, the wise men came from the east to worship him; the people worshipped him, when they cried, Hosanna to the Son of David, blessed is he that cometh in the name of the Lord. And the children praised him, saying Hosanna to the Son of David. These acclamations gave great offence to the chief priests and scribes; they were sore displeased with the children, as they were before, with the multitude; and they said unto Jesus, hearest thou what these say? but Jesus said unto them, yea, have ye never read, *out of the mouths of babes and sucklings thou hast perfected praise?* Praise, therefore, even such praise as God by his grace kindles in the hearts of his children, and teaches their lips to utter, was by babes and sucklings addressed to Jesus Christ: And, shall our lips be silent? Shall children praise the God of salvation; and shall we refuse him the tribute of our praise? Shall we refuse our Hosannas to the author and

finisher

finisher of our faith? The word, Hosannah, signifies, save now I beseech; and shall we not acknowledge Christ's power to save? shall we not praise him who is mighty to save, and who is the author of eternal salvation? The glory of salvation is ascribed to the Son of God, by his ransomed and redeemed; they stand before the throne, and before the Lamb, saying *salvation to our God which sitteth upon the throne, and unto the Lamb.* But the Son is represented as sitting upon the throne, *sitting on the right hand of power;* and it is said that he *sitteth on the right hand of God.* Now if Jesus sitteth on the throne, on his Father's throne, on the right hand of God, and if he said unto the high Priest and the council, *hereafter shall ye see the Son of man sitting on the right hand of power, and coming in the clouds;* then, these words are frequently used to signify the glory, dignity, and bright appearance, of Christ in his exalted state, and in his glorified body. We may therefore in many places consider these words, *sitteth upon the throne,* and, *the Lamb,* as relating to one person. It cannot be denied, that Isaiah saw the Son of God sitting upon the throne, it cannot be denied, that he is the Lamb that was slain, who *after he had offered one sacrifice for sins for ever, sat down on the right hand of God; from henceforth expecting till his enemies be made his footstool.* These words, sitteth upon the throne, and sitting upon the throne, are applicable to the Son of God,

K and

and why may not the praise which is addressed to him that sitteth upon the throne, be considered as addressed to the Son, even to the Lamb, for ever and ever? But at all events, and admitting, that the praise which is addressed to him that sitteth upon the throne, is addressed to the Father, yet the Lamb is also the object of his praise; and when salvation is ascribed to him, is adored as the God of salvation. Salvation belongs to God alone; and the glory of salvation to him only; but this glory is ascribed to the Father, and to the Son Christ Jesus.

Again, *I beheld,* says the Apostle, *and heard the voice of many Angels round about the throne, and the beasts and the elders, and the number of them was ten thousand times ten thousand, and thousands of thousands; saying with a loud voice, worthy is the Lamb that was slain, to receive power, and riches, and wisdom and strength, and honour, and glory, and blessing. And every creature which is in Heaven, and on the earth and under the earth, and such as are in the sea, heard I, saying, blessing, and honour, and glory, and power, be unto him that sitteth upon the throne, and unto the Lamb for ever and ever. And the four beasts said, Amen. And the four and twenty elders fell down and worshipped him that liveth for ever and ever.** And doth not Christ live for ever and ever? Is he not eternal? Is it not one of his glorious titles, that he

* Rev. v. 12, 13, 14.

he liveth for evermore? Do not the Angels and Elders say, glory be unto the Lamb, for ever and ever? Thus the Lamb is worshipped in Heaven by his ransomed and redeemed; and by the Angels of God. The holy Angels delight to do the will of God, and chearfully obey his commandments; and they are commanded to worship the Son: but our God is a jealous God and will not give his glory unto another, and therefore would not have said, let all the Angels of God worship him, that is, the Son, if he was not justly entitled to this worship. It is not an object of power, to command Angels or men to worship one who is not possessed of the divine perfections.

But some will say, where is the use of this commandment given to the Angels? if the Son is God, and consequently, justly entitled to divine worship, would not the Angels have known their duty and have acted accordingly? It is sufficient for us to know, that the infinitely wise God hath commanded the Angels to worship the Son; it is sufficient for us to know, that the giving of this commandment is recorded in the holy scriptures for our instruction. If it is the duty of Angels to worship the Son of God, it is also our duty to do so; it is our duty to honour the Son, even as we honour the Father. Do Angels worship the Son, and shall such creatures as we are, refuse to worship him, at whose name every knee shall

shall bow, before whose judgment seat we must all appear, unto whom we must all give an account, and receive from him, according to the deeds done in the body?

It is recorded, that Jesus was worshipped by his disciples, and that they prayed to him: and of this we have several instances. It is very plain, that the disciples considered him as the hearer of prayer; this says the Apostle, *is the confidence that we have in him, that if we ask any thing according to his will, he heareth us, and if we know that he hear us, whatsoever we ask, we know that we have the petitions that we desired of him.* * The Apostle Paul prayed to the Lord Jesus, to be delivered from some very severe trial or temptation; he calls it a thorn in the flesh, the messenger of Satan to buffet him, lest he should be exalted above measure. Whatever this temptation was, the Apostle had recourse to prayer; and he addressed his prayer unto the Lord Jesus; *I*, says Paul, *besought the Lord thrice, that it might depart from me. And he said unto me, my grace is sufficient for thee; for my strength is made perfect in weakness. Most gladly therefore will I rather glory in mine infirmities, that the power of Christ may rest upon me.* † There are several instances of prayer being addressed to Jesus, while on earth; the disciples prayed to him for increase of faith, the Apostles

* 1. John v. 14, 15. † 2. Cor. xii. 8, 9.

Apostles said unto the Lord, *increase our faith;* and that Jesus was able to do so, was by them acknowledged. But this is the work of God, the work of him who is the head of his Church, and from which head, *all the body, by joints and bands, having nourishment ministered, and knit together, increaseth with the increase of God.** Can Jesus increase the faith of his disciples? then he must be that God who has an absolute command of the human heart, and who giveth grace to the children of men. It is to be observed that Jesus never rebuked any one for praying to him, which, as a teacher sent from God, he would certainly have done, if those that prayed to him, acted contrary to their duty. The disciples prayed to their Lord and Master, when they were exposed to imminent danger in a storm, saying, *Lord save us, we perish.* Let his answer be impressed upon our souls; *he saith unto them, why are ye fearful, O, ye of little faith? Then he arose and rebuked the winds and the sea, and there was a great calm.* Well might the men in the ship marvel; well might they say, *what manner of man is this, that even the winds and the sea obey him?* To rebuke the winds, to make the storm a calm, to still the waves of the sea, is the work of him only, who hath laid the foundations of the earth, who hath set bounds to the sea, and restraineth the

---

* Colossians, ii, 19.

the rage of the great deep: Unto him the diftreffed mariners cry in their trouble, *and he bringeth them out of their diftreffes. He maketh the ftorm a calm, fo that the waves thereof are ftill.* Oh, that men would praife the Lord for his goodnefs, and for his wonderful works to the children of men! *

The act of praying to God, is very frequently in the fcriptures, termed, calling upon God, and upon the name of God: Thus fays the Pfalmift, *I will call upon the Lord who is worthy to be praifed; fo fhall I be faved from mine enemies. In my diftrefs I called upon the Lord, and cried unto my God; he heard my voice out of his temple, and my cry came before him, even into his ears.* Job fpeaking of the hypocrite, fays, will God hear his cry when trouble cometh upon him? will he delight himfelf in the Almighty? *will he always call upon God? Call upon me,* faith the Lord, in the day of trouble, I will deliver thee, and thou fhalt glorify me. And, faith the Prophet, *whofoever fhall call on the name of the Lord fhall be faved.* Hear how the Apoftle applies thefe words of the Prophet; fpeaking of Jefus Chrift, he fays, *Whofoever believeth on him fhall not be afhamed. For there is no difference between the Jew and the Greek; for the fame Lord over all, is rich unto all that call upon him.*† It is very obvious that to call upon God, to call upon the name of
God,

---

* Pfalm cvii.   † Rom. x. 12.

God, is to worship him in prayer. Let us now see if the disciples called upon the name of Jesus. And here we have a very sufficient evidence, besides the passage last quoted. Indeed it appears, that to call upon the name of the Lord Jesus Christ, was the constant practice of the disciples; and that they received a particular denomination from this practice, whether given to them by their enemies, in contempt, or adopted by themselves; but it is certain, they were not ashamed to acknowledge that they called upon his name. Ananias said unto the Lord, who appeared unto him in a vision, Lord, I have heard by many of this man, how much evil he hath done to *thy saints* at Jerusalem; and here he hath authority from the chief priests, *to bind all that call on thy name.* But after Ananias was convinced of Paul's conversion, and that he was a chosen servant of the Lord, he said unto him, arise, and be baptized, and wash away thy sins, *calling upon the name of the Lord.* Hear the Apostle's salutation to the Church of God at Corinth; Paul, called to be an Apostle of Jesus Christ through the will of God, and Sosthenes our brother, unto the Church of God, which is at Corinth, to them that are sanctified in Christ Jesus, called to be saints, *with all that in every place call upon the name of Jesus Christ our Lord both theirs and ours. Grace be unto you, and peace from God our Father, and from the Lord Jesus Christ.*

The

The manner in which the Apostles begin and conclude their epistles, their affectionate salutations, and the divine doxologies which we find so frequently in their writings, are convincing proofs that Christ is the object of religious worship: For we cannot but perceive, that in these salutations, prayer is addressed to Jesus Christ; and that in the doxologies, divine glory is ascribed unto him. Thus for example, *The Lord of Peace himself give you peace always, by all means.—The Lord be with you all.—The grace of the Lord Jesus Christ be with you all, Amen.—The grace of the Lord Jesus Christ and the love of God, and the communion of the Holy Ghost, be with you all, Amen.*—These are prayers, addressed to the Divine persons whose blessings are implored ; they are blessings pronounced in the name of the Lord Jesus, and of the Father, and of the Holy Ghost. It is an act of religious worship, to bless the people in the name of God ; and it is unlawful to bless the people, or pronounce a blessing, but, in the name of him that can confer blessings, and is, himself, the fountain of blessedness. And as to the doxologies used by the Apostles, in them we find divine glory ascribed to Jesus Christ : *To him be glory both now and forever, Amen.—Unto him that loved us, and washed us from our sins in his own blood and hath made us kings and priests unto God, and his Father, to him be glory for ever, Amen.* *

We

---

* Rev. i. 6.

We have already quoted several passages of Scripture, wherein divine glory is ascribed, and divine praise offered to the Son, co-ordinately, with the Father; and shall proceed to shew that the Disciples exercised, and that it is the duty of Christians to exercise, such affections of the soul towards the Son of God, as prove him to be the object of religious worship. To believe in God, to trust in him, to hope in him, and to love him, are true and genuine acts of religious worship. This might be easily proved, but it will not be denied: Let us then enquire, whether we are bound to believe, to trust, to hope in Jesus, and to love him as our God. And first, with regard to faith, it is our duty to believe in Christ; which signifies more than to believe him. It is our duty to believe the Prophets, Evangelists, and Apostles, but we are not said to believe in them. It is our duty to believe Jesus, the great Prophet, and moreover, it is our duty to believe in him; *ye believe in God*, says Christ, *believe also in me*. Here the disciples are commanded to believe in the Son of God; which they would not have been commanded to do if he was not the object of divine faith. This expression, to believe in, is used in the Old Testament, to signify that faith, which the servants of God exercised towards him, and in him; that faith which the servants of God had in their Redeemer, and that faith which believers, in future ages,

should

should have in him : Hear me, O Judah, says Jehoshaphat, and ye inhabitants of Jerusalem, *believe in the Lord your God, so shall ye be established.* The prophet was delivered from the lion's den, *and no manner of hurt was found upon him, because he believed in his God.** And thus saith the Lord, behold I lay in Sion a stumbling stone, and a rock of offence, *and whosoever believeth on him shall not be ashamed.* We are commanded to believe in Jesus, to believe on him, and to believe on his name. Eternal life is promised, yea, Christ himself promised it to them that believe in him ; *He that believeth on the Son of God hath everlasting life ;* and again, *whosoever liveth and believeth in me, shall never die.* God hath commanded us to believe on the name of his Son, and he gave his only begotten Son, *that whosoever believeth in him should not perish, but have everlasting life.* But the nature of this faith in Christ, shews us that it is divine, and has a divine person, even God, for its object. It is a justifying faith, a saving faith, a faith by which Christians overcome the world, and a faith by which they live: The life which I live in the flesh, says the Apostle, *I live by the faith of the Son of God.* Without this faith we cannot be saved, without this faith we cannot please God, we cannot approach unto him as a reconciled God, we cannot glorify him.

Without

---

* Daniel vi. 23.

Without this faith, we can do nothing; for without it we do not abide in Christ; and he hath assured us that we cannot bring forth the fruits of holiness, unless we abide in him; *without me,* says he, *ye can do nothing.* By this faith, Believers rest upon the Lord Jesus for salvation, they believe in him, as the Lord their righteousness, their all sufficient Saviour, who is the end of the law for righteousness, to every one that believeth. In the exercise of faith, Believers trust in the Lord Jesus, and commit their dearest and most important concerns to his care; I know, says the Apostle, *whom I have believed; and that he is able to keep that which I have committed unto him against that day.* The martyr Stephen was stoned, *calling upon God, and saying, Lord Jesus receive my spirit:* * And David committed his soul, and keeping of it, to his God; *into thine hand, I commit my spirit, for thou hast redeemed me, O Lord God of truth.* And the blessed Jesus himself, considered as man, committed his soul to God; *Father, into thy hands, I commend my spirit.* What shall we say then to these things? Did not the Martyr, and the Apostle, commit their souls to the Lord Jesus Christ? Did not David commit his soul to his Redeemer? and does he not call him the Lord God of truth? Is it not sinful,

to

---

* In this text, the word, God, is not in the Original; but the passage is as strong a proof of Christ's divinity without the word.   Acts vii. 60.

to truft in any creature whatever? Can we lawfully truft, and commit our fouls to the care and keeping of any creature? It is the divine prerogative, to keep the foul. He that trufteth in man, and maketh the arm of flefh his confidence, is pronounced accurfed; but it is a duty to truft in God for ever, for in the Lord Jehovah is everlafting ftrength. *Let them that fuffer according to the will of God, commit the keeping of their fouls to him in well doing, as unto a faithful Creator.* It is a fact upon record, that the Apoftle and the Martyr committed the care and keeping of their fouls to the Lord Jefus Chrift; was it their duty to do fo? Is it our duty to imitate their example? If it is, then, we muft acknowledge him to be the object of religious worfhip. Why is Jefus called the Shepherd and the Bifhop of our fouls? Why was it foretold, that the root of Jeffe fhould be for an enfign to the people, that the Gentiles fhould feek to it, and that his reft fhould be Glorious? and what is the meaning of this prediction? the Apoftle informs us, that to feek to Chrift, is to truft in him; *in him fhall the Gentiles truft.* Can there be any reafon given, why we fhould not truft in him? He is *the Author and finifher of our faith; he is able to fave, even to the uttermoft; he is the Author of eternal falvation unto all them that obey him.* It is our duty to keep ourfelves in the love of God, looking for the mercy of our Lord Jefus Chrift unto eternal life;

And

And what kind of truſt, are Believers to exerciſe towards him, by whoſe mercy they are to obtain eternal life, and by whoſe grace they are ſaved? How are we to truſt in and reſt upon that Lord and Saviour, whoſe grace is ſufficient for us, whoſe ſtrength is perfected in weakneſs, who giveth unto his ſheep everlaſting life, and aſſures them, that they ſhall never periſh? It is a divine, holy, and religious truſt, that is to be repoſed in him, unto whom we commit our precious and immortal ſouls; and in whom we truſt for ſalvation through his mercy. The Apoſtle truſted in Chriſt, that he would providentially order and over-rule events relative to the edification of the Church; *I truſt in the Lord Jeſus Chriſt, to ſend Timotheus ſhortly unto you. I truſt in the Lord, that I alſo myſelf ſhall come ſhortly.* This is an acknowledgment of his providential Government.

I have had occaſion, in the former diſcourſe, to ſay ſomething concerning our hope in Chriſt. I refer you to what has been there ſaid concerning the *God of Hope*, the *Hope of Iſrael*, the *Hope of glory*, and the hope that we have in Chriſt, who is called, *Our Hope.* We proceed to ſhew, that to love the Lord Jeſus, as we are commanded to do, is an act of religious worſhip. It will not be denied, that it is our duty to love the Lord Jeſus Chriſt; the only queſtion is this, how are we to love him? I anſwer,

answer, we are to love him more than we love our neighbour, more than we love our nearest and dearest relations, more than we love ourselves, more than we love our lives. To shew the greatness of this love to Christ, it is even called an hating of all our nearest relatives, and of our own lives. The words are figurative indeed, but they are very strong, and expressive of the intensity of that love, with which we should love our Lord and Saviour: *If any man come to me,* saith Christ, *and hate not his father, and mother, and wife, and children, and brethren, and sisters, yea, and his own life also, he cannot be my disciple.** What manner of love is this? If a disciple must thus love Christ, if he must love him more than all his nearest and dearest relations, then he must love him with all his heart, with all his soul, and with all his mind. But this is that love which is required, in the first and great commandment; *Thou shalt love the Lord thy God with all thine heart; and with all thy soul, and with all thy mind.* Thus it is that we are to love God; and we are to love our neighbour as ourselves. The distinction between our love to God, and our love to our neighbour, is very obvious: It is not our duty to love any Being but our God, more than we love our neighbour, our nearest and dearest relations, and even our own lives; but, thus, it is our duty to love

* Luke xiv. 26.

love the Lord Jesus. For his sake, it is our duty to lay down our lives, if in the course of divine providence, we should be called to suffer for him and his cause, rather than deny him. *Be thou faithful unto death,* saith the Lord Jesus, *and I will give unto thee a crown of life.* And again, *whosoever will save his life, shall lose it ; and whosoever will lose his life for my sake, shall find it.* Who shall separate us from the love of Christ? Shall tribulation, or distress, or persecution, or famine, or nakedness, or peril, or sword? These calamities, were no proof that Christ did not love his suffering disciples, did not separate them from his grace and love ; nor could these dreadful afflictions force the disciples to deny Jesus. Their love, through grace, was proof against these attacks; *as it is written, for thy sake we are killed all the day long ; we are accounted as sheep for the slaughter ;** nay, *in all these things we are more than conquerors through him that loved us.* And again in the book of the Revelations, it is said, that they overcame their enemy, the evil one, *by the blood of the Lamb, and by the word of their testimony ; and they loved not their own lives unto the death.*† What manner of love is this? It is our love to that Saviour, who died for us, and whose love to us passeth knowledge. How are we to testify our love to God? By keeping his commandments;

This

* Rom. viii. 36. † Rev. xii. 11.

This is the love of God that we keep his commandments. How are we to testify our love to Christ? by keeping his commandments; *if ye love me*, says Christ, *keep my commandments. He that sayeth I know him, and keepeth not his commandments, is a liar, and the truth is not in him. But whoso keepeth his word, in him verily is the love of God perfected.*

I shall conclude this discourse, with some observations upon the ordinances of baptism and the Lord's Supper; for in these ordinances the Lord Jesus is religiously worshipped. They prove that he is the object of religious worship; and this proves that he is our Lord, and our God. And what is baptism? Is it a civil institution? or is it a holy ordinance, a religious rite, a Sacrament of the New Testament, a sign and seal of the new covenant? For our present purpose it is sufficient to consider Baptism, as a religious ordinance instituted by the Lord Jesus Christ: Indeed, as to the present argument, it is sufficient that it is a religious institution, the observance of which, is enjoined in the word of God; and that in the celebration of this ordinance, God is obeyed, honoured, and worshipped. If the Father is worshipped in this ordinance, how is he worshipped? The person who administers Baptism, and the person baptised, if adult, and the believing parent dedicating his child to God the Father, in the bonds of his holy covenant, acknowledge

ledge him to be their God, and profess their faith and hope in him. If to baptize, or to receive baptism in the name of God the Father, is an act of religious worship; what is it, to baptize, or to be baptized in the name of the Son, and in the name of the Holy Ghost, are there three distinct baptisms, one, in the name of the Father, who is acknowledged to be the true God, and is to be worshipped; and two other baptisms, in the name of two persons, not divine, and therefore not to be worshipped? The Christian baptism, is one; and is administered in the name of the Father, and of the Son and of the Holy Ghost. In this ordinance, according to the words of Institution, these names are used conjointly, and co-ordinately; it is not lawful to omit the name of the Father, or the name of the Son, or the name of the Holy Ghost: and if these names must be used conjointly, they must be used co-ordinately. The question, at present, is this; is there any act of religious worship exercised towards the Son? is he worshipped in this ordinance? I answer that he is; because it is unlawful to baptize in the name of one who is not the object of religious worship. The Apostle abhorred the idea of baptizing in his own name; *was Paul crucified for you? or where ye baptized in the name of Paul? I thank God, that I baptized none of you, but Crispus and Gaius, lest any should say, that I had baptized in* *mine own name**. If it should be objected, that the children of Israel were *baptized unto Moses, in the cloud and in the sea*; let it be observed, that Moses was a type of Christ, and that this baptism in the cloud and in the sea, was typical. The word, Baptism, does not always signify a religious institution to be observed by the Church; it sometimes signifies a particular dispensation of divine providence. The children of Israel were all under the cloud, and all passed through the sea, and were all baptized unto Moses, in the cloud, and in the sea. By this dispensation of divine providence, Israel was taught to consider Moses as the person that God had raised up and appointed to be their leader; and were encouraged to follow him, as one having a divine commission to bring them out of the land of their captivity. But will any one say, that the children of Israel were baptized unto Moses, as we are baptized into Christ? where they baptized in the name of Moses? did they *put on* Moses, as Christians *put on* Christ? were they *baptized into his death?* was Moses crucified for them? or was he the author and finisher of their faith? Moses was not that spiritual meat, of which all Israel eat; nor was he that spiritual rock, of which all Israel drank; but Christ was. The Lord Jesus Christ is the bread of life; and that spiritual rock of which Israel drank; *that rock was Christ.*† But, to bring this matter to a short

---

* i. Cor. 1. 14.   Cor. x. 3, 4.

a short issue; we are either bound to worship Chr'st in this ordinance, or we are not; if not, why is his name used objectively in a religious ordinance? and why did Ananias exhort Paul to be baptized, and to wash away his sins, *calling upon the name of the Lord?* If Christ is to be worshipped in this ordinance; is it an inferior worship that he is intitled to? It is not. This is evident, from the nature of religious worship; and made level to every capacity, by an express revelation of the Divine will; namely, *that all men should honour the Son, even as they honour the Father.* Religious worship, in a certain sense, admits of degrees, some are by grace enabled to worship more fervently, and with more exalted affections, than others are; but as the object of religious worship is infinitely perfect, infinitely glorious, and infinitely worthy to be worshipped; there cannot be any worship to which he is not intitled.

With regard to the Sacrament of the Lord's Supper, let it be considered as a religious commemorative institution, and this is the very least that can be said of it, unless we take it to be a human invention, or a state Test to be used in qualifying for civil offices. I do not mean to inquire, by what authority the Lord Jesus Christ instituted this ordinance; nor to argue from his being the Institutor, in favour of his divinity: all that is necessary for our present purpose, is, that the Lord's Supper is a religious commemorative ordinance. And who will deny that it is? That it is a very solemn ordinance of our holy religion, will not be denied by any one that pays due regard to these words of the Apostle: *As often as ye eat this bread, and drink this cup, ye do shew the Lord's death till he come. Wherefore, whosoever shall eat this bread, and drink this cup of the Lord, unworthily, shall be guilty of the body and blood of the Lord. But let a man examine himself, and so let him eat of that bread and drink of that cup. For he that eateth and drinketh unworthily, eateth and drinketh damnation,* or, as the word may be rendered, JUDGMENT *to himself, not discerning the Lord's body. For this cause many are weak and sickly among you, and many sleep.** This ordinance of our holy religion, is commemorative; *do this*, saith Christ, *in remembrance of me.* The person who is commemorated in a religious ordinance, is religiously commemorated. And what is religious commemoration? It is religious worship, a duty which we owe to God alone. The end of religious commemoration, is thanksgiving; *sing unto the Lord, O ye saints of his, and give thanks at the remembrance of his holiness. Return, O Lord, deliver my soul, Oh! save me for thy mercies sake. For in death there is no remembrance of thee: In the grave, who shall give thee thanks?* If thanksgiving is the chief end of religious commemoration,

* 1. Cor. xi. 26.

moration, then, the Lord Jesus Christ, who is religiously commemorated in the Lord's Supper, is to be praised with thankſgiving, for his redeeming love. To what purpoſe do we ſhew forth his death? to what purpoſe do we remember him? to what purpoſe do we commemorate his dying love, over the Symbols of his body broken, and his blood ſhed for the remiſſion of ſins, if we do not acknowledge him to be our redeeming Saviour, and if we do not praiſe him with thankſgiving? Is it not our duty to praiſe the Lord Jeſus, at his table, and to give thanks at the remembrance of his loving kindneſs and his tender mercies? *unto him that loved us and waſhed us from our ſins in his own blood, and hath made us kings and prieſts unto God and his father, to him be glory and dominion for ever, Amen.*

SERMON FOURTH.

John 20th Chap. 28th Verse.

And Thomas answered and said unto him, my Lord and my God.

IN this discourse, I will endeavour to give a general answer to objectors.

The objections to the doctrine of the Divinity of our Lord and Saviour, are neither so numerous, nor so various, as some are apt to imagine; they are all reducible to two classes, and are derived from two sources, Reason, and Revelation: We do not mean that either Reason or Revelation affords any solid foundation for these objections; but objectors appeal to Reason, or to Revelation, and most generally to both, and consider these as the foundation of their objections and arguments.

As to objections of the former clafs, before we yield to their force, we fhould be affured that we have carefully and impartially confidered the fubject; and that thefe objections are, either, felf evident propofitions, or juft conclufions, drawn from clear, evident, and rational premifes, and not *oppofitions of fcience, falfely fo called, which fome profeffing, have erred concerning the faith.* But above all, we fhould remember that the light of nature, or human reafon, is not competent to decide againft the truth of any doctrine, which it could not difcover, and which when revealed, it cannot comprehend; provided, this doctrine contains in it nothing abfurd or contradictory to reafon. The human mind is not omnifcient; our knowledge, at beft, is limited, and the entrance of fin into the heart has impaired our faculties, at leaft with regard to things fpiritual and divine: but granting that this is not the cafe, and that the human mind is in as high a ftate of perfection as ever it was, yet certainly there may be many things which human reafon cannot find out unto perfection.

If any perfon fhould advance a myfterious doctrine, and acknowledge that it is not revealed in the word of God; if it does not contradict my reafon, nor the word of God, it may be true, for any thing I know; but the queftion is, have I fufficient evidence that it is true. If another perfon fhould advance a myfterious

ous doctrine, and assert that it is contained in the holy scriptures; then it is reasonable that I should consult the sacred records, with a view to find out the truth or falsehood of this assertion; and if this doctrine is not contained in the scriptures, my faith is no way concerned in it, even though the doctrine should not be contradictory to reason.

Again, if a certain doctrine should be advanced, as a mysterious doctrine contained in the word of God, and if I could perceive that this doctrine, instead of being a divine mystery, was a palpable absurdity, I might safely conclude that it had no foundation in the word of God. But if some person should advance a mysterious doctrine, and if upon searching the scriptures, I find this doctrine clearly revealed; I may safely presume that it is neither contradictory to reason, nor to that general revelation; of which it is a part. If upon the strictest examination, I cannot find in this doctrine, any thing contrary to reason; and as the doctrine may therefore be true, so, being revealed in the word of God, it must be true: and as to passages of the same general revelation, which may seem to be in opposition to the doctrine, it is my duty to endeavour to reconcile them to the doctrine, in such a manner as shall produce a perfect harmony; which can be effected, with regard to the doctrine of Christ's divinity and with great facility. A doctrine which is clearly revealed

in

in the word of God, is not to be denied, given up, or explained away, on account of some passages of scripture, which may seem to militate against it; for the opposition may be only apparent, not real.

I presume it will not be denied, that Jesus Christ, the Son of the Virgin Mary, was really and truly a Man. This is a truth frequently asserted in the sacred scriptures, and cannot be denied. Nevertheless, this same Jesus has divine attributes ascribed unto him; is called JEHOVAH; is called God; is called King of Kings and Lord of Lords; and is the object of religious worship. Shall we therefore deny that Jesus Christ is really and truly a man? This we cannot do without contradicting the scriptures, and without denying an established and indubitable fact: If then, divine attributes, divine names and titles ascribed, and divine worship paid unto Jesus, are not sufficient to warrant us to deny his humanity; why should the attributes of sinless humanity, warrant us to deny his divinity? Are these two propositions, viz. Christ is God, and Christ is man, contradictory? If we admit the first, must we reject the latter? or if we admit the latter, must we reject the former? By no means; we are under no such necessity. It is not contradictory to reason, to say that Christ is both God and man; but unless we admit this proposition to be true, we are under the necessity of charging the scriptures with self-contradiction

diction and must give up either one or other of these doctrines: We must give up the scriptures, as records that cannot be depended upon.

This doctrine of the hypostatic union, namely, that the Lord Jesus Christ is both God and man, and yet but one person, one Christ, is not contradictory to reason. It is indeed a great mystery; it is the great mystery of Godliness. It is not contradictory to reason, to assert that a man is a being consisting of soul and body; but this also is a great mystery.

But some may say, what have we to do with mysteries? I answer, much more than many are willing to acknowledge. There are mysteries in the Christian religion, which are revealed, declared and made known unto us in the sacred scriptures; and if we acknowledge the scripture to be the word of that God who does nothing in vain, we must confess that these mysteries were revealed to answer some important purpose, with regard to the glory of God, and the interest of our immortal souls.

Are there no mysteries in the natural world? yes, there are facts, there are many things which we cannot fully understand nor find out unto perfection: There are many things too high for us, and which say unto our understandings, thus far and no farther. And this we experience in our search after the knowledge of natural things, when we attempt to investigate the causes of things, the connexion between cause and effect, and the manner how the cause acts in producing its proper effect. There are natural mysteries; and the Philosopher is not ashamed to pay particular attention to these things, nor to write his thoughts and publish his discoveries to the world; these writings are read with pleasure, and they contribute to increase our knowledge, while at the same time they teach us this humiliating lesson, that, comparatively, we know nothing, or that the things which we know are very disproportionate to the things that we do not know. What man can explain the nature of his soul's connexion with his body; or the manner how the soul acts upon his body, and is acted upon? How does spirit act upon matter? It is a mystery to me at this moment, how an act of my will moves the muscles of my hand in writing; and it must be a mystery to the reader, how, by means of the eye, his mind is made acquainted with my thoughts: for though words are marks or signs of ideas, and are agreed upon as such, yet these questions remain unanswered, namely, what is the connexion between a visible mark and a thought of the mind, or how does an Image of the mark upon the retina, produce thought? What is the connexion between thought and the expansion of the optic nerve? There are mysteries innumerable, in the natural world; and there are

mysteries

mysteries in the moral world: We find them in natural religion, in God's moral Government, and in the dispensations of Providence. It may therefore be presumed, that in revealed religion, and in the dispensations of grace, there are mysteries which, if revealed religion is of high importance, are highly important. If natural religion cannot be without mysteries, because God is Infinite and cannot be found out unto perfection, revealed religion must contain mysteries, for the same reason.

As Revelation contains several doctrines which the light of nature could never have discovered; so it is highly reasonable to conclude, that in these doctrines there may be something mysterious; and that reason, which could not make the discovery, may not be able to comprehend the whole of these revelations or revealed doctrines. May there not be some doctrines which we cannot comprehend when revealed, as well as doctrines which we could not find out without revelation?

As God is infinite and therefore, incomprehensible; as his judgments are *unsearchable*, and his ways *past finding out*; a revelation from God, relative to Himself and his unsearchable judgments, must contain mysteries. But to shew clearly, that there are mysteries in the Christian religion, I shall produce several instances. First, the resurrection of the body, is a doctrine of revelation, and it is a
mysterious

mysterious doctrine. No man will venture to say that he is able to comprehend how God raises the dead body, any more than he comprehends how God caused him to be conceived in the womb; but God has declared that the dead body shall be raised immortal; this mortal must put on immortality, and this corruptible must put on incorruption.

There is certainly something mysterious in the doctrine of the resurrection; for says the Apostle, *behold, I shew you a mystery; the dead shall be raised incorruptible, and we shall be changed.* Here are many things we cannot find out unto perfection: we cannot tell the nature of that change which those who shall not sleep, shall undergo at the coming of the Lord Jesus; but God knows it, and it should not be thought an incredible thing that God should raise the dead body or change the living.

The relation of Christ to his Church, is a mystery, *a great mystery;* yet it is asserted that he and his Church are one body. Have we nothing to do with this mystery? Or are we not to believe it, unless we are able to understand or explain the precise nature of this connexion? We know some reasons why Christ and his Church are called one body mystical; there may be other reasons which none but omniscience knows; but if divine wisdom had given us no reason in this matter, the declaration of the Apostle is sufficient to ascertain the fact, namely, that

that Christ and his Church are, in a certain sense, one body.

In the dispensations of grace, revealed religion shews us mysteries, as natural religion shews us mysteries in the course of divine Providence. The Apostle asserts that blindness in part, happened unto Israel, until the fulness of the Gentiles be come in; and that this was a wise dispensation of God; I am certain it was a mysterious one, and that it is one of those ways of God which are past finding out. *I would not brethren*, says the Apostle, *that ye should be ignorant of this mystery, lest ye should be wise in your own conceits, that blindness in part is happened unto Israel, until the fulness of the Gentiles be come in.* Here is a mystery of which the Apostle would not have his brethren ignorant, therefore something may be known concerning mysteries; he would not have them ignorant of the fact, though the divine procedure in this matter is inscrutable; as appears in the conclusion of this chapter, where the Apostle resolves the whole of this dispensation, into the wisdom, the knowledge, and sovereignty of God; *O the depth of the riches both of the wisdom and knowledge of God! how unsearchable are his judgments, and his ways past finding out! For who hath known the mind of the Lord, or who hath been his Counsellor? Or who hath first given him, and it shall be recompensed unto him again? For of him, and through him,*

and

and to him are all things; to whom be glory for ever, Amen.*

This myftery was not declared or made known to the church merely for fpeculation, but to fhew the vanity of human wifdom, to prevent the difciples from being wife in their own conceits, and to teach them humility. This fame Apoftle fpeaks of *his knowledge in the myftery of Chrift;* and in the clofe of his epiftle to the Romans he ufes thefe remarkable words, *now to him that is of power to 'ftablifh you, according to my gofpel, and the preaching of Jefus Chrift, according to the revelation of the myftery, which was kept fecret fince the world began; but is now made manifeft, and by the fcriptures of the Prophets, according to the commandment of the everlafting God, made known to all nations for the obedience of faith.*† Whoever ferioufly attends to thefe words of the infpired Apoftle, will fcarcely venture to affert that we have nothing to do with myfteries in religion; feeing a myftery has been revealed by the commandment of the everlafting God, *for the obedience of faith.*

In the facred fcriptures, there are doctrines revealed which the light of nature could never have difcovered; but when revealed or made known, they appear perfectly agreeable to the dictates of found reafon, admirably fuited to our fituation and neceffities, and every

---

* Romans xi. chap. † Romans xvi. 25, 26.

every way worthy of a Wife, Holy, Juſt and Merciful God. Theſe doctrines may be called myſteries, becauſe the light of reaſon could never have diſcovered them; they may be called the hidden things which revelation hath diſcovered, more obſcurely or myſteriouſly in the days of the Fathers, and of the Prophets, but with clearer and ſtronger light in the goſpel of Chriſt; and they may ſtill with propriety be called myſteries, becauſe in theſe doctrines which reaſon approves, and faith rejoices to believe, there is an height, to which our moſt elevated thoughts cannot ſoar, a length and breadth we cannot meaſure, and a depth which is unfathomable.

The ſame ſcriptures contain ſome doctrines which are more highly myſterious than others; there are leſſer and greater myſteries in the chriſtian revelation; we can ſee farther into ſome than we can into others, and theſe are the greateſt myſteries, in which reaſon is leaſt concerned, and faith moſt. With regard to doctrines above reaſon, divine faith, which is the ſubſtance of things hoped for, and the evidence of things not ſeen, reſts upon the teſtimony of God, and believes upon the authority of the holy ſcriptures, doctrines which reaſon cannot comprehend.

But it will be aſked what are we to believe? Can we believe any doctrine or propoſition evidently above our comprehenſion? or can we aſſert or deny any

any propofition concerning fuch matters? Yes, we can fay that God is Eternal and Infinite, yet, God, Eternity, and Infinity, are incomprehenfible. We can fay that we have fouls, and that they act upon our bodily organs, and are affected by thefe organs, but we cannot comprehend how. We know that there is a God, but that he is unfearchable; we know that he has exifted from all eternity and never began to exift; here our faculties are loft in an unfathomable abyfs. We may believe more than we can know, or there can be no fuch thing as faith; all things that can be known by us, are the objects of the underftanding; things that cannot be fully known, or are above our comprehenfion, are, when revealed, the proper objects of faith. In every fcripture myftery, there is fomething of which we can form clear and diftinct ideas; there is always fomething clear, plain, and intelligible, while at the fame time there are other things not fo clear, and others that are perfectly incomprehenfible by us. We will endeavour to illuftrate this in a particular cafe, and by an inftance which is directly in point. The Apoftle, writing to Timothy, fays, *without controverfy great is the myftery of Godlinefs ; God was manifeft in the flefh, juftified in the fpirit, feen of Angels, preached unto the Gentiles, believed on in the world, received up into glory.** In the firft place,

it

---

* 1. Timothy, iii. 16.

it is very obvious, that there is one great myftery in the Chriftian revelation; without controverfy, fays the Apoftle, great is the myftery of Godlinefs. Secondly, the Apoftle afferts certain facts, and it is plain that he had fome ideas of thefe facts, fome ideas annexed to the words which he ufed in his epiftle, and that Timothy, to whom he wrote, might have fome ideas of the Apoftle's words; and confequently, that we who have this epiftle to read, may alfo have fome ideas of the facts recorded. God was manifeft in the flefh; God was juftified in the fpirit; God was feen of Angels; God was preached unto the Gentiles; God was believed on in the world; and God was received up into glory: All thefe propofitions are contained in the text; and they are true, if the word of God is true. I fhall confine myfelf to the firft propofition, namely, God was manifeft in the flefh; and whatever this may mean, it is evident that God was manifeft in the flefh, either in a way and manner that we can comprehend, or in a way and manner that we cannot comprehend; but, that he was manifeft in the flefh, cannot be denied.

We have fome clear and diftinct ideas of God, though none that are adequate to his nature and perfections; and we have fome clear and diftinct ideas of the word, flefh; and thus we may form this propofition: viz. God appeared in the flefh,
that

that is, in our nature. The Apostle Paul says, that he was seen of Angels; and the Apostle John says, he was seen of men. This person who appeared and was seen in our nature, is God the Son; for he is the person who was justified in the spirit, preached unto the Gentiles, believed on in the world, received up into glory.

Farther, the Apostle John says, *the Word was made flesh, and dwelt among us; and we beheld his glory, the glory as of the only begotten of the Father, full of grace and truth.* Hence it follows, that he who was manifest in the flesh, was made flesh; now as it is absurd to suppose that the divine nature could be changed into the human, therefore, we must have recourse to other passages of scripture, relating to the same subject, for more light and information in this matter; for these words, *made flesh;* cannot possibly signify, that the divine nature was made the human nature, or changed into it. Upon further inquiry, we find, that the scriptures speak more fully and clearly upon this subject; and we are informed, that the Son of God took upon him the form of a servant, that he was possessed of the divine nature, that he was in the form of God, and thought it not robbery to be equal with God; that he made himself of no reputation, took upon him the form of a servant, and was made in the likeness of men. I shall quote the whole passage, as it will ascertain some very important facts which will help
to

to determine what meaning we are to annex to the words above mentioned. *Let this mind be in you, which was also in Christ Jesus: Who being in the form of God, thought it not robbery to be equal with God; but made himself of no reputation, and took upon him the form of a servant, and was made in the likeness of men: and being found in fashion as a man, he humbled himself and became obedient unto death, even the death of the cross.* * Here, the form of a servant signifies the nature of a servant, the human nature, for this was the nature Christ took upon him, if he took any nature upon him: We know that he did not take upon him the nature of Angels, but we know, that *forasmuch then as the children are partakers of flesh and blood, he also himself likewise took part of the same.* We know, that *he took on him the seed of Abraham;* we know that he *was made like unto his brethren;* we are assured that he was really and truly man, the Son of Mary, and descended from the fathers of the Jewish nation, and *made of the seed of David according to the flesh.* Here, the word, flesh, signifies the human nature; and this is the nature which Christ took upon him, when he took upon him the form of a servant. The form of a servant, therefore, signifies the nature of a servant, in the passage above mentioned; for Christ was not the semblance of a man, he was really and truly man; and whoever
denies

* Philippians ii. chap.

denies that Christ is come in the flesh, that is, in our nature, is an anti-christ, as saith the Apostle. If then, the *form of a servant* signifies the nature of a servant, and this nature is the human nature, which, and which alone, Christ took on him, why must the word, *form*, in the first clause of the verse signify any thing less than nature? the form of God is evidently the nature of God; and this explanation of the word, which is absolutely necessary, with regard to the form of a servant, is as necessary with regard to the form of God. It is clear therefore, that Jesus Christ the Son of God, was in the form of God, before he took upon him the form, the nature of a servant, the human nature; and as he who is possessed of the divine nature, can never be dispossessed of it, never can change this nature; so, by taking upon him the form of a servant, he did not cease to be a divine person, that is, God: But as we cannot comprehend, how he has taken the human nature into personal union, and as we cannot conceive the manner and nature of this union, we confess, that the incarnation of the Son of God is an inscrutible mystery, one of those things that omniscience alone can perfectly know; and we join with the Apostle in acknowledging, that *without controversy, great is the mystery of Godliness; God was manifest in the flesh.* But would it not be impious, and irrational to say, there is no such thing as the mystery of Godlinefs, or that it is not a great mystery,

tery, or that God was not manifest in the flesh, because we cannot comprehend the precise nature of this manifestation? God can do many things that we cannot comprehend; he has done many things, in the works of nature, providence, and grace, that are truly mysterious; his works are wonderful, his judgments are unsearchable, and his way past finding out. The words which the Lord spoke to his servant Job, out of the whirlwind may be confessed to every one who rejects the mysteries of God, because he cannot understand them perfectly: *gird up now thy loins like a man, for I will demand of thee and answer thou me. Where wast thou when I laid the foundations of the earth? declare if thou hast understanding. Who hath laid the measures thereof if thou knowest; or who hath stretched the line upon it whereupon are the foundations thereof fastened, or who laid the corner stone thereof?* And again, *hast thou entered into the springs of the sea? or hast thou walked in the search of the depth? have the gates of death been opened unto thee: or hast thou seen the doors of the shadow of death? hast thou perceived the breadth of the earth? declare if thou knowest it all. Where is the place where light dwelleth? and as for the darkness, where is the place thereof; that thou shouldst take it to the bounds thereof, and that thou shouldst know the paths to the house thereof? Knowest thou it because thou wast then born, or because the number of thy days is great? hast thou entered into the treasures of the snow? or hast thou*

seen

seen the treasures of the hail, which I have reserved against the time of trouble, against the day of battle and war? By what way is the light parted, which scattereth the east wind upon the earth? Who hath divided a water course for the overflowing of waters? or a way for the lightning of thunder, to cause it to rain on the earth where man is; on the wilderness wherein there is no man; to satisfy the desolate and waste ground, and to cause the bud of the tender herb to spring forth? Hath the rain a father? or who hath begotten the drops of the dew? Knowest thou the ordinances of Heaven? Canst thou set the dominions thereof in the earth?

But farther, the great mystery of Godliness is asserted by the Apostle, in the following words: viz. *whose are the fathers, and of whom, as concerning the flesh, Christ came, who is over all God blessed for ever.* Here, Christ is said, in a certain sense to be descended from the Patriarchs; this sense is a restricted and particular one; he descended from the fathers of the Jewish nation, *as concerning the flesh,* as to his flesh, or his human nature, and that nature only. He therefore had another nature, according to which, as has been already observed, he did not descend from them; and this is that nature in virtue of which, he is called the ever-blessed God.*

Here,

---

* It has been shewed in a former discourse, in what sense Christ is called God. If it should be considered as an objection to the doctrine then delivered, that the article before the

Here, we may give a satisfactory answer to some important questions which our Lord asked the Pharisees, but which they could not answer; *while the Pharisees were gathered together, Jesus asked them, saying, what think ye of Christ? whose son is he? They say unto him the Son of David.* This answer, in a certain sense, was true: But Jesus said unto them, *how then doth David, in spirit call him Lord?* And again, *if David then call him Lord, how is he his Son? And no man was able to answer him a word, neither durst any man, from that day forth, ask him any more questions.* But a believer, though only a babe in Christ, can easily answer these questions which were too hard for the Pharisees, who were wise in their own eyes, and thought that wisdom would die with them. A Christian can say, that Christ was the Son of David, that is, descended from him, as concerning

---

word God, in the original language, is not always used when the Son is called God; I answer, that it is several times used, and this is sufficient; for if it is a distinguishing mark of true and proper Deity, then it should never have been prefixed to the word, God, when it relates to the Son, if he is not really and truly God. As to supreme and subordinate Deity, sound reason, as well as scripture, rejects the Idea. But it is perfectly unaccountable, why men of learning should lay such stress upon the article, which, from its minuteness might be, and I doubt not, was sometimes forgotten by transcribers. How can we consider the article as a mark of true Deity, when we find that the article is used in that passage, where the Devil is called the God of this world!

concerning the flesh; and that David under the influence of the spirit, called Christ his Lord, and thereby acknowledged him as his God. *The root of David,* that is, the Creator of David, was in a certain sense the *offspring of David.* After what has been said concerning mysteries, and the great mystery of godliness, in particular, I presume it cannot be denied that there are two distinct natures in the Person of Jesus Christ. In fact, though this doctrine is mysterious, yet it is clearly revealed in the word of God; and we are obliged by necessity to admit of its truth. What necessity? The necessity of reconciling one part of Scripture to another, which, without this doctrine, cannot be done: But this doctrine, in conjunction with another, namely, that the Lord Jesus Christ is Mediator between God and man, reconciles one portion of Scripture to another, and effectually harmonizes the language of inspiration.

To say that man is immortal, and that man is mortal, is no contradiction; we use this mode of speaking, and do not consider ourselves guilty of any absurdity, or, even impropriety of speech. Why so? because, the soul of man is immortal, and his body is mortal; and therefore, very different things may be affirmed of one man, yea, things that would be palpable contradictions, if man did not consist of soul and body. It is easy to perceive, that the first proposition asserts that man is immortal, as to his

his soul, and the second, that man is mortal as to his body. In like manner, there are many things said of our Lord Jesus Christ, which must be considered as directly contradictory to each other, if we do not admit both his Divinity and his humanity; but admitting this doctrine, and that of his Mediatorial Character and office, it is easy to reconcile all the terms of inferiority and of subordination, in which he is spoken of with those which assert his Divinity, and of course, his equality with the Father.

But it will be said, that the names, Father, and Son, are sufficient to shew that the Son is inferior to the Father; we answer, that before this Objection can have any weight, it must be proved that these names have the same signification when applied to God and his only begotten Son, that they have when applied to men. But this cannot be done, except in one instance, namely, that the Son has the same nature his Father has; and to assert this we are warranted, nay, obliged by Scripture. It has been proved that the Son is possessed of the Divine perfections, and, consequently, of the Divine nature; in this nature there cannot be any imperfection, and therefore the Son cannot be inferior to him that is all-perfect. As far as we can reason upon this subject from analogy, and that is no farther than the Scripture allows us, the argument is in our favour.

If

If the Son's *obligation to obedience*, is not founded in his being the eternal and only begotten of the Father; if from his Sonship, we cannot infer his obligation to obedience, then why should we infer his inferiority, from his being called the Son? Christ's obligation to obey, arose from another source, as it is plain from the following Scripture; viz. *Though he were a Son, yet learned he obedience by the things that he suffered.* These words might be better translated, *though he was Son.* Now, if his obligation to obedience was founded in his Sonship, the above words would, I presume, be absurd; for instead of the adversatives *though*, and *yet*, the words, because, and therefore, would have been proper. Let it be remembered, that the Jews understood these names, Father, and Son, to signify the equality of the persons so denominated: for when Christ called God his Father, the Jews said that he made himself *equal with God.* And when he said, *I and my Father are one*, they again took up stones to stone him for Blasphemy, because said they, that thou, being a man, makest thyself God. Jesus was so far from retracting what he had said, or explaining himself to the satisfaction of the Jews, that his last words, on this occasion viz. I am in the Father, and the Father in me, were as offensive as the former; *therefore they again sought to take him, but he escaped out of their hands.* The Sonship of Christ is a great mystery: his generation

tion is eternal, and incomprehenſible, therefore ineffable : but this we know, that Jeſus is the Only begotten of the Father; that he is the brightneſs of his glory, and the expreſs Image of his perſon; and that he and his Father are one.

SERMON FIFTH.

John 20th Chap. 28th Verse.

And Thomas answered and said unto him, my Lord and my God.

THE sacred Scriptures were written for our instruction, and to make us wise unto Salvation. The doctrines of the everlasting Gospel, are sacred, sublime, and saving truths, every way worthy to be received and believed; they are faithful sayings and worthy of all acceptation, and under the Influence of Divine Grace, will make us wise, religious, and happy.

Among these doctrines, the great mystery of godliness appears with peculiar glory; and from its high importance, and its connection with other

doctrines

doctrines of revelation, and with true practical religion, may be justly considered as the main pillar of our most holy faith.

The doctrine of Christ's divinity is a practical doctrine; and to shew its connexion with practical religion, or its practical use, is the design of the following discourse.

First, this doctrine is connected with practical religion, and is of practical use, because it is connected with the most solemn exercises of devotion; at all events, it deserves our most serious consideration, that if it be true, we may receive and embrace it as the truth of God, or if it be false, we may reject it; but it is of infinite importance to be rightly informed in this matter; for religious principles are of the highest importance; and to be mistaken, as to the object of our faith and worship is, at least, awfully dangerous. The doctrine of Christ's divinity is either true or false; if it be true, as it certainly is, then we must believe it and exercise our faith and hope accordingly, that is, we must believe in Jesus, we must trust in him, and love and serve him, in the obedience of faith; yea, we must honour him as we honour the Father; but if Christ is not God, then we must not believe in him, nor trust in him, nor worship him, nor pray to him, nor honour him as we honour the Father. This makes a great difference in practical religion

religion, in faith and practice. Principles are intimately connected with practice; yea, religious principle is religious practice, in several instances, where no outward act of religion is exercised. The seat of religion is in the heart, in the thoughts, purposes and affections of the mind; and the outward acts of religion spring from the affections of the soul. Thus for instance, our religious principles are our religion, when, under the pressure of great afflictions, we consider them as coming from the hand of God, as a fatherly chastisement; from the hand, I say, of that God who loves and pities his children, does not afflict them willingly, and has promised that all things shall work together for good to them that love God. Upon these principles, namely, our firm persuasion and conviction that there is an over ruling Providence, and that God doth always that which is right, that he is good and gracious, and that he can and will cause all things to work together for good to them that love him, our minds quietly submit and resign to the dispensations of God, hope in his mercy, and confide in his promises. These acts of religion, are all acts of the soul, and movements of the heart towards God.

The doctrine we have been defending, is no speculative doctrine, it contains principles intimately connected with the religion of the heart, which is practical religion. And these principles are also connected

with

with the outward acts of religion, if inward religion and the outward exercises of devotion and worship are, or ought to be connected. If this doctrine be false, they that believe it to be true and in consequence of this persuasion, address one prayer to Christ, or sing his praises, or exercise towards him any act of religious worship, are idolaters; and of consequence the Apostles were idolaters, and the Saints and the Angels are idolators, or the Scriptures are not the word of God, nor given by the inspiration of the holy spirit. But if the doctrine be true, what are they who reject it, and will not give glory unto the Son of God, the glory due unto his holy name? What are they who will not acknowledge the Son of God, as their Lord and their God? they are unbelievers and Children of disobedience. Again, to shew the connection of this doctrine with practical religion, we observe, that it is intimately connected with an act of practical religion, namely, our drawing nigh to God through a Mediator, by whom we have access, to a reconciled God and Father. If the doctrine of Christ's divinity is not true, then there is no access to God, no way of drawing nigh to God, no opportunity to exercise this religious duty: For, if Christ is not the Redeemer, the Mediator, the way, the truth, and the life then there is no Redeemer, no Mediator, no access to the Father, for no man, saith the the Scripture, cometh to the Father but by him. Now, if there is no access by him, then there is no

access

access at all. But if Christ is not that Redeemer, that Mediator which the Scripture declares him to be, then he is not the Mediator by whom we should have access to the Father; that is, if he does not answer the exact account and description given of him, as the Mediator by whom we are to have access to God, then the access to God, is not by him, but perhaps by another; however, we know that there is but one Christ, one Mediator, one Redeemer, and if Jesus is not this Christ, this Redeemer, then all our hope in him is lost and perished. Christ Jesus is not the Redeemer spoken of in Scripture, if he is not God manifest in the flesh. He is not the Redeemer, if he is not *the maker, the husband of his Church, the Holy One of Israel, the Lord of Hosts, the God of the whole earth.* He is both God and man, who Mediates between God and man; the Mediator must be able to lay his hand upon both parties, and reconcile them to each other. I mention this to shew that if we give up the doctrine of Christ's divinity, we give up our hope of salvation by Jesus Christ. The intercession of men and Angels is utterly insufficient to save us; let none lean upon that broken reed: the true intercessor is he who can save to the uttermost, whose arm can bring salvation, whose intercession can never fail, and who is *the Lord our righteousness.*

Secondly,

Q

Secondly, let us practically improve this doctrine, for the strengthening of our faith in the Son of God; let us say with the Saints of God, we know whom we have believed; We do not trust in an arm of flesh for salvation, but our trust, hope, and confidence is in the living God. The mighty God of Jacob is our refuge, our strong rock and fortress. Let each of us say, with David, *The Lord is my Shepherd I shall not want. He maketh me to lie down in the green pastures; he leadeth me beside the still waters. He restoreth my soul; He leadeth me in the paths of righteousness for his names sake. Yea, though I walk through the valley of the shadow of death, I will fear no evil, for thou art with me, thy rod and thy staff they comfort me.* Is our Faith weak? Or are we of little faith? We may, if we believe the doctrine of Christ's divinity, apply to Jesus for increase of every grace; we may say unto him as the disciples did, *Lord increase our faith;* we may say unto him, *Lord we believe; help thou our unbelief.* If we deny the divinity of the Son of God, we cannot consistently approach him in prayer: we cannot say with the Apostle, *this is the confidence that we have in him, that if we ask any thing according to his will he heareth us. And if we know that he hear us, whatsoever we ask, we know that we have the petitions that we desired of him.** If we believe as the Apostles did, in Jesus, we may have the same kind of

---

* 1 Ep. John v. 14. 15.

of confidence that they had; we may with them pray to Jesus, and trust in him as the hearer of prayer. If we are beset with temptations, if thorns in the flesh, messengers of Satan, are sent to buffet us, we may beseech the Lord, that they may depart from us; and he that heard the Apostle will hear us, and either deliver us from the temptations, by removing them, or he will afford us sufficient strength to resist them. His grace is sufficient for us; his strength is made perfect in weakness. Are we weak in ourselves? in Christ we have strength and are made strong, yea, able to do all things through his strength; *I can do all things, says the Apostle, through Christ which strengtheneth me.* In the belief of this doctrine of our holy faith, we have an holy confidence towards God the Father, as a reconciled Father, and a comfortable assurance that he will hear and graciously answer the prayer of faith, addressed to him in the name of Jesus; he presents the prayer of his people, their spiritual offerings and sacrifices unto the Father, perfumed with sacred incense, being our great high Priest who ever liveth to make intercession for us; him the Father heareth always, and in him he is always well pleased. But if we deny the divinity of our Mediator, advocate, intercessor, and high Priest, we can have no reason to hope that the Father will hear our prayer, in fact, we do not pray through the Mediator, and our prayers are not the prayers of faith, if we do not depend

upon

upon the intercession of our great high Priest; and how can we depend upon his intercession, if he be but a man, or an Angel?

Thirdly, let us improve this doctrine of our holy faith, to the confirmation of our hope of eternal life, that so we may have good hope through grace, as the *anchor of our souls both sure and stedfast, and which entereth into that within the vail, whither the forerunner is for us entered, even Jesus, made an high Priest forever, after the order of Melchisedec.** Eternal life is the highest and most glorious object of hope, and this eternal life is in the Son of God; it is the gift of God through Jesus Christ. *This,* says the Apostle, *is the record that God hath given to us eternal life, and this life is in his Son, he that hath the Son hath life, and he that hath not the Son of God hath not life. These things have I written unto you that believe on the name of the Son of God, that ye may know that ye have eternal life, and that ye may believe on the name of the Son of God. And again, we know that the Son of God is come, and hath given us an understanding that we may know him that is true: and we are in him that is true, even in his Son Jesus Christ, this is the true God and eternal life.*† If we cannot believe that the Son of God is the true God, if the Apostle erred, in saying that he is the true God, may he not have

erred

---

* Heb. vi. 19.   † 1 John v. chap.

erred in saying that he is eternal life? how can we depend upon the record above mentioned, *God hath given us eternal life, and this life is in his Son?* If the Son is not the true God, what dependance can we have upon the Scriptures? And what hope can we have in Christ, as the giver of eternal life, and the bread of life, if he is not the true God?

The doctrine of Christ's divinity establishes the hope of believers, even their hope of eternal life, upon a solid foundation; they behold in Jesus the Son of God, an all-sufficient, an Almighty Saviour; they can say with the Psalmist, in God is our salvation and our glory, the rock of our strength and our refuge is in God. And as this doctrine establishes the hope of believers, so it is the source and spring of their spiritual consolation; they that believe in the Son of God, as their God and Saviour, as the Lord their righteousness, and as their compassionate Redeemer, may well be filled with all joy in believing in the Son of God. The great mystery of godliness pours the balm of consolation into the wounded heart, and troubled soul, God was manifest in the flesh, and we know that *he was manifested to take away our sins, and in him is no sin** was God manifested in the flesh? was he manifested to take away our sins? and can the sacred and blessed

---

* 1. John iii. chap.

blessed work fail in his hands? Is the great Immanuel the Redeeming Saviour? did he die for us? did he redeem his Church with his own blood? Was he who knew no sin made sin for us, that we might be made the righteousness of God in him? who then shall lay any thing to the charge of God's elect? who shall condemn us, if God justifies us? who shall impute sin unto us, if Christ has redeemed us from the curse of the law, by being made a curse for us, and by having borne our sins in his Body on the tree? *Who shall lay any thing to the charge of God's elect? it is God that justifieth: who is he that condemneth? It is Christ that died, yea, rather, that is risen again, who is even at the right hand of God, who also maketh intercession for us.*

Come then sinner, come in faith, and adore the mercy of thy glorious Saviour; come and lay thy sins and guilt at the foot of his cross; come to Jesus for salvation, for pardon, for righteousness, and for sanctification; He is the very Saviour you want; In him all fulness dwells; he is able to save even to the uttermost, all that come to the Father by him. Jesus will not refuse you his salvation; he will not cast out those that come to him: he will not break the bruised reed, nor quench the smoaking flax; he will bind up the broken hearted and comfort all the mourners in Zion: *If any man thirst* says Christ, *let him come unto me and drink;*
he

he that believeth on me, as the Scripture hath said, out of his belly shall flow rivers of living water; and elsewhere, whosoever drinketh of the water that I shall give him, shall never thirst; but the water that I shall give him, shall be in him a well of water springing up into everlasting life.* Jesus can pour down upon his people the sacred influence of his holy spirit, and fill our souls with divine consolation, light, and love.

Fourthly, let us improve the doctrine practically, to the increasing of our love to God the Father, and to the Son Christ Jesus. The love of the Father appears most conspicuously in his unspeakable gift; in this was manifested the love of God towards us, because that God sent his only begotten Son into the world that we might live through him. Herein is love, not that we loved God, but that he loved us, and sent his Son to be the propitiation for our sins.† The Father hath given us eternal life, and this life is in his Son; He gave us his well beloved Son, the brightness of his glory, and the express image of his person; he gave us his Son in whom he delighted from all eternity, yea, for our sakes, he spared not his own Son, but delivered him up to the death for us all. Though God consulted his own honour and glory in this stupendous dispensation, yet divine love and compassion shine forth with transcendent lustre, and

---

* John vii. chap. † 1st Ep. John iv. chap.

and brightness; in this dispensation, we see that *God is love*. Had God sent the highest Angel in Heaven, to save us, (if salvation could be the work of an Angel) this would have been great love; but, *herein is love, and in this* was manifested the love of God, because that God sent his only begotten Son, that we might live through him. When Abraham by faith offered up his only Son Isaac, the Angel of the Lord said unto him, now I know that thou fearest God, seeing thou hast not withheld *thy Son, thine only Son, from me;* the stress is laid upon those words, thy Son, thine only Son; as this was the highest act of Abraham's faith, fear, love, and obedience, so, God's giving his own Son, his only begotten Son, his well-beloved Son, is the greatest act and most glorious manifestation of divine love, love unspeakable and incomprehensible. So great is the love of God in giving us his own Son, that upon this manifestation of love, the Apostle builds his hope of receiving from the God of love, every needful grace and blessing. *He that spared not his own Son, but delivered him up to the death for us all, how shall he not with him also freely give us all things?* Every blessing, every precious gift of God to his Church, here, and hereafter grace, glory, and eternal life, are all summed up in this one unspeakable gift of God, his own Son Christ Jesus. If our love to God is to be excited by a believing view of his love to us, *if we love him because*

he

he firſt loved us, then that doctrine which gives us the brighteſt and moſt glorious view of divine love to ſinners, muſt, as a practical doctrine, have the ſtrongeſt tendency to excite and encreaſe our love to God; and therefore muſt be moſt practically uſeful; but no doctrine can ſhew the love of God to ſinners in ſuch a glorious point of view, as the doctrine of the incarnation, life, ſufferings, and death of the Son of God.

And for the encreaſing of our love to Jeſus, our compaſſionate Saviour, let us conſider, that he who loved us and waſhed us from our ſins, in his blood, is the Son of God, the brightneſs of the Father's glory, and the expreſs image of his perſon. The true way to encreaſe our love to Chriſt Jeſus, is to dwell with ſacred delight and rapture upon his love to us; and the true way to eſtimate his love, if love unſpeakable can be eſtimated, is to view the dignity and glory of him who loved us, and maniſeſted his love in his divine condeſcenſion, and in his lowly humiliation. The love of Chriſt *paſſeth knowledge:* it is unſpeakable and incomprehenſible, becauſe it is the love of God manifeſt in the fleſh. *Hereby,* ſays the beloved diſciple, *perceive we the love of God, becauſe he laid down his life for us;** that is, hereby we perceive the love of God the Son, becauſe he condeſcended to be incarnate, to take upon

* John iii. 16.

upon him our nature, to be made of the seed of David according to the flesh, to be born of a Virgin; and finally to give his life a ransom for many, to redeem them from the curse of the law, the wrath of an offended God, and eternal misery. In this view, the love of Jesus appears indeed to be that which passeth knowledge, and to be truly ineffable and divine. The grace of our Lord Jesus is the grace of him that was rich, and for our sake became poor; and this is the argument which the Apostle uses when he exhorts the disciples to abound in the grace of love; *ye know the grace of our Lord Jesus Christ, that though he was rich, yet for your sakes he became poor, that ye through his poverty might be rich.**

Behold then the Son of God, rich in all the glories of godhead and divinity, possessed of the divine nature and divine attributes; behold him in the bosom of the Father; behold his divine condescension, in his becoming surety for sinners; behold him in this character, and hear him utter these gracious words, lo; *I come, in the volume of the book it is written of me, I delight to do thy will O God; By which will,* says the Apostle, *we are sanctified by the offering of the body of Jesus once for all.* Behold the Son of God, in his birth, life, sufferings and death; remember who he is that endured so much for sinners; remember

* 2. Corinth. viii, 9.

remember that he is the great Immanuel, God with us, and admire with sacred rapture and delight, the wonders of redeeming love! Unto him that loved us and washed us from our sins in his own blood, and hath made us Kings and Priests unto God and his Father, to him be glory and dominion for ever, Amen.

Lastly, let us practically improve this doctrine, the great mystery of Godliness, unto holiness of life: that so we may adorn *the doctrine of God our Saviour* in all things; and if we would adorn the doctrine of our Saviour, we must believe that he is our God. The practice of true holiness, of pure and undefiled religion, does not begin in unbelief; obedience does not commence with disobedience to the express command of God the Father, who hath commanded us to believe in his Son: but how do they believe in the Son who deny *the Lord that bought them, and bring upon themselves swift destruction.** Can Antichrist be religious and holy? can a liar love truth? and *who is a liar?* faith the Apostle, *but he that denieth that Jesus is the Christ? He is Antichrist that denieth the Father and the Son; whosoever denieth the Son, the same hath not the Father.* He is Antichrist and a liar who denieth that Jesus is the Christ, that is, the Messiah; but he that denies the divinity of Jesus, denies that he is Christ, the Anointed, the Messiah:

for

* 2 Peter, ii. 1.

for if he is not God, neither is he Messiah, the Messiah is *Immanuel,* God with us. He that hath the Son, hath life, and he that hath not the Son hath not life; now he that denieth the Son, hath not the Son, nor the Father, and has no life, but is dead in trespasses and sins.

True believers experience a sacred constraining influence in the love of Jesus Christ; *the love of Christ,* says the Apostle, *constraineth us because we thus judge that if one died for all, then were all dead; and that he died for all, that they which live should not henceforth live unto themselves, but unto him which died for them, and rose again.* Believing in this Saviour as their God, they truly perceive his love, and this is the language of their souls, *hereby perceive we the love of God, in that he laid down his life for us.* In this faith they behold the glory and riches of Redeeming love, and feel its peculiar constraining energy. In the great mystery of godliness, the believer beholds not only the love of God to sinners, in giving his Son to be their Saviour, but also the holiness of God, and his abhorrence and detestation of sin. In the death of the Son of God, as the surety and representative of sinners, the purity and holiness, the righteousness and justice of God, are most gloriously illustrated and displayed, as well as his grace and mercy. How infinitely merciful, holy, just, and righteous is our God, who in his infinite

finite love gave us his Son to be the propitiation for our fins! He would not pardon finners, without vindicating the honour of his holy and righteous law; he would not be reconciled to finners, but by the death of his own Son, who hath magnified the divine law and made it honourable. How inflexible is divine juftice! behold this attribute of God in the fufferings and death of Chrift! behold, how God vifited his own Son, as the finners furety! in his Pity and in his love he gave him to us, to be our Saviour; but the fword of his juftice is drawn againft him; *awake O fword, againft my Shepherd, and againft the man that is my fellow, faith the Lord of Hofts; fmite the Shepherd.* God fpared not his own Son, *it pleafed the Lord to bruife him; he hath put him to grief. He was wounded for our tranfgreffions, he was bruifed for our iniquities; the chaftifement of our peace was upon him, with his ftripes we are healed. The Lord hath laid on him the iniquity of us all. He was oppreffed and he was afflicted, yet he opened not his mouth; he is brought as a lamb to the flaughter.* Behold the Son of God, in his life, his fufferings, particularly his laft fufferings in the garden and on the Crofs! behold his agony and bloody fweat! hear him fay, Father fave me from this hour, but for this caufe came I to this hour. O, my Father, if this cup may not pafs away from me except I drink it, thy will be done. Hear him crying out on the Crofs,

Cross, my God, my God, why haſt thou forſaken me? Behold theſe things, and be aſtoniſhed at the terrors of Divine juſtice; and admire the riches of redeeming love! If God thus viſited his own dear Son, conſidered as ſurety for ſinners, ſhall not God viſit with everlaſting deſtruction, all the impenitent workers of iniquity? if theſe things are done in a green tree what ſhall be done in a dry? ſhall not the divine wrath flame out againſt all who are not in Chriſt; againſt all who are not ſaved from wrath by him: againſt all who are not waſhed in the atoning blood; againſt all who are not cloathed with his righteouſneſs? where ſhall they fly for refuge, who would not have Chriſt to be their Saviour, nor their Lord to reign over them? what will become of them? they ſhall go away into everlaſting puniſhment, and be deſtroyed with an everlaſting deſtruction. In the doctrine of Chriſt's divinity, as connected with the doctrine of the atonement, we behold as in a mirror, the love and mercy, the truth and faithfulneſs, the holineſs and juſtice of God: we behold the glory of his grace, and the awfulneſs of his wrath; we behold the dignity and honour of his laws, and have every motive laid before us to fly to Chriſt for ſalvation, to believe in, and to reſt upon him for eternal life. The Son of God gave himſelf for us, that he might redeem us from all iniquity, and purify us unto himſelf a peculiar people zealous of good works: let us then live unto him who died for us,

and

and rose again; who died for our offences, and rose again for our justification. Let us testify our love to him, by keeping his commandments: they are the commandments of our Lord and Saviour, who is entitled to our submission and obedience, because he is our God, our Redeemer and our King. Let us worship and adore him; let us praise and bless his holy name; let his word dwell richly in us; let his law be our delight; and let all that love his salvation say continually the Lord be magnified.

FINIS.

www.ingramcontent.com/pod-product-compliance
Lightning Source LLC
Chambersburg PA
CBHW020109170426
43199CB00009B/464